One dollar from the purchase
of each copy of this book is being donated
to S.H.A.R.E. Agricultural Foundation.
A hand up, not a hand out.

I am a great fan of the work that S.H.A.R.E. does in Central and South America. This organization has an impact on a tremendous number of lives, increases the benefits through the "pass-on" principle, and isn't burdened with large administration costs.

This is a volunteer-driven registered charity, in the purest sense of it.

To learn more about S.H.A.R.E, go to shareagfoundation.org
or contact them at:

1756 Countryside Dr.
Brampton, Ont. L6R 0B6
1 888 337 4273

To my mom, Connie

God bless you.

Mak

Acknowledgements

While I will take responsibility for every word in this book, I cannot take full credit.

My thanks go to a number of people:

To my friends at Home Hardware for encouraging me to write this book.

To my editor Karen York, with whom I work at *Gardening Life* magazine, for not only sharing her editing skills in an honest and helpful way but also encouraging me to go down new paths with my writing that I may not have explored otherwise.

To my assistant Brenda Hensley for her patience and attention to detail. Her ability to handle my last-minute demands for research and review of the facts has helped to bring a measure of accuracy to this book that would not otherwise exist.

To Ron Mugford, the highly talented graphic guru from Home Hardware, who added to his already overburdened work schedule to put this book together in a form that makes sense and looks appealing.

To David Cleary of Lone Pine Publishing, who made sure the technical aspects of publishing the book were properly taken care of.

To Macie Hunt for appearing with me in the cover photo. She is an impressive kid who acts so naturally in front of the camera. Plus, she likes to garden!

To my kids Ben, Emma, Heather and Lynn, who all deserve a big hug for inspiring me to write this book. It is for you as much as it is about you. I hope you enjoy the family stories that I used for both illustration and information.

To my wife Mary who inspires me, encourages me and is a fabulous mother to our kids. How can I thank you enough?

To all the other people who play important roles in this book: my mom Connie and late father Len, my friends in my PAG, my radio listeners and TV viewers. Many are featured in these pages—please know that if you are one of them, I am most thankful for your contribution.

Photo: Heather Cullen

Mark Cullen
www.markcullen.com

National Library of Canada Cataloguing in Publication Data

Mark Cullen
a Sandbox of a different kind

Includes index

ISBN 978-0-9782665-0-9

First printing 2007

Printed in Canada by Friesens

a Sandbox of a different kind

Contents

Introduction

My mother likes to remind me that she spent the first half of her child-rearing years teaching her kids how to get along in life and the second half learning from them. This book is an acknowledgement that I passed the halfway mark when my youngest child, Ben, turned 10.

I had spent a lot of time dreaming about the beautiful garden I would one day create in my backyard and looking forward to the experience of actually doing it. In the meantime, I watched Ben in his sandbox and wondered how he could spend seemingly endless hours moving sand around, building gas stations and running his miniature cars and trucks up ramps and along imaginary roads without any regard for the more serious issues in life. The answer clearly was, "Because he's a kid!" I was beginning to learn from my kids. Lesson #1—take time to play.

A Sandbox of a Different Kind is a book full of lessons that I have learned, not just from my kids but also from other family members, friends and the many gardeners I have met in my 25 years as a garden communicator. It is full of observations, too—of the garden that I cultivate and the greater gardening world around us. It acknowledges the frustrations of gardening in a harsh climate like Canada and brings to light many of the advantages we enjoy here, too. Its contents are intended to inform and entertain anyone who enjoys the experience of active gardening or simply takes pleasure in looking at the horticultural fruits of someone else's labour.

While this book is based on my own personal reflections of the gardening experience, I like to think of it as a celebration of our collective horticultural history. As with all history lessons, this one encourages us to consider where we are in our particular chapter of gardening history and to look ahead.

We live in exciting times, with limitless potential to change our world quickly and for the better. I believe the garden provides a glorious opportunity for all of us to make meaningful and lasting changes.

Mark Cullen

www.markcullen.com

Thus, We Are Rich

CHAPTER 1

"Don't just get caught up in keeping up."
Anonymous

There's an old expression that "a hedge between makes friendship green." The idea is that if we create a thin barrier between our neighbours and ourselves—but not too great a barrier—we can enjoy all the benefits of living in our private space while growing a neighbourly relationship with...well, our neighbour. There's a reason you didn't move into a commune, right?

This friendship is even greener with neighbours who share an interest in gardening. Take, for instance, the habit many of us have of sharing plant material. You may have some perennials in your garden that have matured to the point that they need to be dug up and divided. Well, you can either replant them elsewhere around your yard or share them with a neighbour.

Digging up and dividing plants as gifts for others has been going on for generations. Long before there was a garden centre or mass merchant with an excessive inventory of plants on almost every corner, gardeners relied on each other to "grow" their gardens. A clump of peonies, a little bundle of daylilies or a lilac cutting, carefully wrapped in moistened paper and placed in a bag, would be handed over the fence or left on the doorstep of a neighbour or friend. It was a rite of spring and a rite of autumn, too. It was not just a friendly gesture but also a terrific way to gain some control over an otherwise overgrown garden.

Of course, we don't do this with next-door neighbours exclusively; check out your local garden club or horticultural society and you'll find there's a whole lot more sharing going on at their meetings than outsiders imagine. The members visit one another's gardens, borrow tools and not only adopt plants but, in the extreme, become godparents to each other's kids. Although these days we seem to acquire more plants from retailers than we do from each other (not necessarily a bad thing), I suggest we truly value the plant exchanging that does go on. Not just the plant, but the experience.

Look at your gift of a hosta or a daylily division as a deposit in your bank account of friendship building—to be withdrawn on a rainy day, when you are feeling down or need someone to buy chocolate almonds to support your kids' hockey team. We don't need to be buddy-buddy with our neighbours. Just neighbourly is good enough. And that is where the "hedge between" comes in.

Giving gifts of perennials reminds me of my dad's very favourite poem, one that he committed to memory while in his teens. It's called "My Neighbour's Roses" and was written by Abraham L. Gruber:

The roses red on my neighbour's vine
Are owned by him, but they are also mine.
His was the cost, and his the labour, too,
But mine as well as his the joy,
their loveliness to view.

They bloom for me and are for me as fair
As for the man who gives them all his care.
Thus, I am rich because a good man grew
A rose-clad vine for all his neighbours' view.

I know from this that others plant for me,
That what they own my joy may also be;
So why be selfish when so much that's fine
Is grown for you upon your neighbour's vine?

"My Neighbour's Roses"
Abraham L. Gruber

A Honey Bee's Heartbeat

"Go slowly."

James A. van Sweden
Landscape Architect

H ere is a concept that many non-gardeners have trouble grasping: flowers were created for only one purpose and it has nothing whatsoever to do with us. Rather, it has everything to do with sex—plant reproduction, that is.

Blossoms are produced to attract pollinators—hummingbirds, butterflies, moths and of course honey bees, all of which play a vital role in this drama that Mother Nature wrote and puts on every year in our gardens. It has been playing since the beginning of time. All of creation depends on it. So Mom N. does her best to put on a show and, from the May flowers to the last rose of autumn, the advertising is out there for all to see.

But the target audience is not you and me.

Stop on a windless day while in your garden and listen. I mean really listen. You may hear the wind as it moves through your garden. Or the sound of a songbird. And maybe you will hear the heartbeat of a honey bee. Okay, maybe you won't. But you could very well hear the buzz of its wings.

Now here is the interesting thing—the buzzing of the bee's wings and the vibration of its body literally rattle the pollen off the anther of the flower while the clever little pollinator negotiates itself as deeply into the flower as possible.

This maximizes the amount of pollen the bee can gather on its mission. As the bee makes its rounds from bloom to bloom, the pollen is spread and the flowers fertilized.

Once pollination has taken place, the flower withers and dies so the plant's energy can go into the production of seed, which of course is meant to produce another plant. In other words, those poppy seeds on your bagel were taken, like the coconut, the banana and the black pepper, for our own use without regard for their intended purpose. Not to make you feel guilty or anything—chances are there will be plenty of poppy seeds to go around for everyone, with little danger that poppies will become extinct.

Back to your garden for a moment—sit still for a while and it is amazing what you will hear and smell and see....the sounds, scents and sights of a garden in transition, which it surely is always and forever. Much of this activity in our gardens, as passive as it seems, is clear evidence that plants are making babies.

So admire your flowers' alluring beauty and breathe in their perfume, knowing that, like so much of what we hear and see these days, the message boils down to sex.

As a Cook Sees a Great Meal, I See A Garden

"I appreciate the misunderstanding I have had with Nature over my perennial border. I think it is a flower garden; she thinks it is a meadow lacking grass, and tries to correct the error."

Sara Stein
My Weeds; A Gardener's Botany (1988)

CHAPTER 3

I t is early May and the gorgeous flowers on my indoor passion vine remind me of the beautiful blooms of summer yet to come in my garden.

In the meantime, there is a brown-grey pall lying among the shrubs and emerging perennials. It is called dirt by many well meaning but less-than-serious gardeners. Now is the ideal time to enhance that "dirt" with generous quantities of compost. The results are guaranteed to be better than if you just let everything be.

Here we are on the threshold of a great gardening season and it shocks me how many experienced gardeners do not seem to understand the opportunities that lie at our feet, quite literally, this time of year. Give me the kitchen scraps and yard waste of the neighbourhood and I will give you gardener's gold—platinum in fact. It will just take some time. It is called compost.

Much the same way that a good cook will look at a table of fresh meat and produce and see in her mind's eye a fabulous meal, I will look at a pile of rotting organic "waste" and envision a gorgeous garden. Give me those raw ingredients and I'll give you glorious blooms, bugs (good ones) and birds to beat the band.

The fallen leaves of last autumn are still on the surface of the soil in my garden, waiting for the earthworms, those great foot soldiers of the yard, to move up to the surface, pull them down, digest them and leave behind nitrogen-rich castings.

When asked, as I frequently am, how best to test garden soil, I say, "Dig a few holes in your garden and count the earthworms. If you have lots, you have healthy soil. If you don't, then you had better add a couple of inches of finished compost to enhance the quality of the existing soil and to feed your worms."

You may ask, "How do I know if I have lots of earth-worms?" I am not sure how to answer that question except to say that *Organic Gardening* magazine estimated that the average North American yard harbours about six tons of these precious critters. You can do the math from there. I will never have enough earthworms in my garden for my liking.

Here's the lesson: over 90 percent of the success that you enjoy in your garden is the result of proper soil preparation. It ain't sexy, I know. But as you get into it, you will come to like it— both the activity of producing great soil and the look, feel and smell of it. But all of this comes with time and experience. Be patient, my friend, be patient. And in time you may fall in love with the concept of converting leftovers into something very useful indeed, as I have. You may even start taking the raw ingredients for your compost from the end of your neighbour's driveway on leaf-pick-up day. That can be kind of fun too.

If you now think I am totally crazy, the line-up starts over there behind my kids who just happen to share your opinion.

For more information on composting visit:
www.markcullen.com
www.compost.org

Simplifying the Message

"As for me, I will let my garden do the speaking."
Anonymous

I picked a single rose the other day and floated it in a coffee mug. Hardly an elegant thing to do, but you know, it did the trick. The rose blossom was a surprise anyway, as the bush that it came from is "out of bloom." I just wanted to enjoy it indoors where I could see it more readily.

My mom has always appreciated a single rose above all. My dad would sometimes come home with a fistful of fresh long-stemmed roses from the rose garden at his public show garden, Cullen Gardens and Miniature Village, in Whitby, Ont. He could afford to do this as he had over 2,500 rose bushes growing at one time. Mom was always a little lukewarm to the idea. Before any time had gone by, she had given all but one away to visitors and friends. She would say, "Just give me one rose. It's all that I can enjoy at one time."

In Victorian times, there was a whole language created around flowers, and many books were written about it—I have quite a few of them in my antique gardening book collection. It was the Victorians who decided that the red rose was a sign of passion and the white rose a signal of unity. A carnation signified divine love, while a violet was taken as a sign of faithfulness. You get the idea.

Every February around Valentine's Day there is all kinds of press about the language of flowers but frankly, I don't know of anyone who has sent a bouquet to a friend or lover without a written note. We just don't speak the language any more. It may be more accurate to say that we use more words than is necessary. I receive some e-mails that ramble on for so long I wonder if the writer just needs something to do. There are "blogs" that specialize in going on and on. Not necessarily with any reason either.

And the rambling voice mail is one of my greatest pet peeves, especially the ones that end by giving the return phone number in such haste that it sounds like an afterthought. "Give me chance to write it down!" I want to scream.

I'd like to suggest that we take the time to think of ways to communicate without wasting a lot of words. Let's begin with the premise that a rambling dissertation on any subject can lose the listener's attention. We can work from there.

Start by picking just one flower and putting it in a prominent place in the home. Or give a single bloom to a friend without saying anything more about it. The receiver of the gift will be left to interpret the message, and that has to be a good thing, don't you think?

As my mom says, "You were given two ears and one mouth for a reason."

So let the gift do the speaking.

The Sandbox

"But though I am an old man, I am but a young gardener."

Thomas Jefferson
Letter to Charles Willson Peale, August 20, 1811

CHAPTER 5

My son Ben was about eight years old when he announced that I could have the space in the backyard dedicated to his sandbox just as soon as he turned 13. Funny how our kids seem take ownership of our real estate, even at such a young age.

Time passed. I would look out of our living room window every winter and dream about the very special garden that I would someday create in that shady corner of the yard. I would extend my woodland garden theme and build a stream that would tumble down a slope into a deep pond filled with fish happily chowing down on mosquito larvae. They would be colourful fish that I could view from the window. It would be gorgeous. I could relax down there and shed the worries of a workday amid the sounds and sights of my own backyard retreat.

The only thing standing in my way was a 3.6-by-3.6-metre (12-by-12-foot) sandbox sitting right in the middle of my scheme.

I became restless and, when Ben turned 11, I said to him, "You know that sandbox? I've been watching and I don't think you used it more than once last year. How would you feel if I took the space over?" To which he replied, "And what would you do with it?"

Now anyone who knows me also knows that I love my garden. I enjoy being in it and shaping it, helping it to evolve over time. I thought everyone knew that I love gardening. But my son—the one guy I live with day in and out—couldn't figure out what I might want with his claimed piece of the family backyard. So I didn't answer him directly. Instead I said, "I am going to build a sandbox of a different kind." And a smile grew across his face like a dawning light.

"Okay, sure," he said. Simple as that. Three winters of dreaming were over; it was time for action. So the next spring I dug in. It was a particularly difficult spring in our business, and I remember coming home from work and escaping to my backyard project. On my knees, dirt up my elbows—the sandbox came out, a large load of triple mix came in. I brought home plants, plants and more plants and then I installed the waterfall and pond, just as I had imagined.

Then I added the fish. Nothing fancy, just colourful goldfish that glinted in the sun as I looked out the window. My dream was complete. The only task remaining was to nurture the rhododendrons, evergreen ground covers and the native plants that I had planted along my woodland walk. It was working out there in my new garden that I came to think of my entire gardening experience as my own personal playtime. To a very large degree, I was enjoying an activity that was not a whole lot different from what Ben enjoyed in his sandbox.

The concept of "garden as sandbox" has changed my point of view on gardening. By definition, both are places for recreation and fun—a great reminder when I take my garden too seriously.

A sandbox is a place to create and build; it provides the opportunity to be an artist, knowing that your work will generally disappear with time, rain and weather. A garden is no different. It is a creative endeavour that is always a work in progress. Nature sees to that as plants grow, mature and die. The whole system of the garden is in flux.

I think the 11 years that I spent looking out our living room window, dreaming of using Ben's sandbox space as a garden, was not time wasted. As I watched him completely engrossed in his activity, I realized I have a lot to learn about play.

Gardeners Live Longer

"Gardening is...an outlet for fanaticism, violence, love,
and rationality without their worst side effects."

Geoffrey Charlesworth
A Gardener Obsessed (1944)

T he obituaries in the newspaper this morning included the most extraordinary story about a woman by the name of Letha Mae Seaman who lived to 107. Imagine. 107.

Letha Mae met her first and only husband before the First World War. They married in 1920 and had four children; they were married for 59 years before he died. Then Letha Mae lived for another 27 years. Wow.

But here is the most interesting part. I quote directly from the newspaper, "During WWII, Letha took it upon herself to knit and sew hundreds of articles for the armed services. She was an avid housekeeper and, to the envy of her neighbours, was a meticulous gardener."

Now I think that it would be misleading to suggest that gardeners live longer, especially when there is only anecdotal evidence that this may be true. I am reminded that the founder of our family firm, John Weall, lived to his 100th year in reasonably good health. But living to a ripe old age is perhaps not the best reason to carry on gardening. I'm a proponent of the "quality of life" argument. I believe that we garden not to live longer but to improve and maintain our quality of life while we are here. As long as we are active in the garden and living on the earth, it is not such a bad idea to do it with a good appetite, some flexibility in the limbs and a sound night's sleep: all of which can result from our gardening activities. And if we happen to live longer as a result, that's not so bad, right?

Notice that Letha Mae was a knitter. So is my wife Mary, and I mean a big-time, passionate knitter. If we both live to 107, we will have been married for 82 years.

That thought may be enough for Mary to take up smoking any day now.

Diversity in the Garden

"And the Lord God planted a garden eastward in Eden."
—Genesis 2

I have nothing against plant hybridizers. In fact, many of the plants in my line of Mark's Choice plants come from suppliers of the latest hybrid introductions. But I think it is wrong to fill our gardens with the trend-setting plant varieties and push aside many of the stand-bys that are proven garden performers in their own right.

Take tomatoes, for example. Last year I grew 200 plants. I had lots of tomatoes—lots of *different* tomatoes. And most of them were hybrids, to be sure. My favourite is Park's Whopper, a Park Seed variety that produces the ideal hamburger tomato. Perfectly round, big as a softball, resistant to cracking even in rainy weather, and tasty as all get out. Really.

But I only eat so many hamburgers. About four plants are plenty for our family of six—and that's assuming all the kids are around, which is not a sure bet now that they are of driving age. I plant a wide variety of tomatoes including some heritage (or heirloom) varieties. These are plants whose parentage goes back a long, long way—their genetics are "pure" and haven't been monkeyed with by human hands. Unlike hybrids, heritage plants come true—that is, if you sow the seed from last year's crop, you will get the same variety this year.

According to an article in Macleans magazine,* there is a swelling of interest in heritage seed varieties, and outfits such as Salt Spring Seeds will make sure that these tried-and-true varieties are available to us all.

As a rule, heritage tomato varieties are tastier than the new hybrids. Mary Brittain of The Cottage Gardener, a family-run heirloom seed and plant nursery in Newtonville, Ont., says, "Heirloom varieties have distinct, discernible flavours. Some have a smoky taste while some are very sweet and others are more acidic. Whatever the taste, it hits you and it lights up your taste buds. It's something you're eating to enjoy on its own."

Compared to the winter tomatoes that you find in the supermarket, there is just no comparison. Garrison Keillor, host of *A Prairie Home Companion*, says that our winter tomatoes are "strip-mined" in Texas or California. He has a point. These are "frankentomatoes," bred to be shipped long distances without bruising, losing colour or by some miracle becoming flavourful. Where frankentomatoes are extremely consistent in colour and shape (which allows for mechanized harvesting), heirloom tomatoes are often lumpy and asymmetrical—but less likely to roll off the table.

So why don't I just grow a full crop of heritage varieties? Because they are prone to disease, crack in the heat and the wet and are more susceptible to early blight than the hybrids that I enjoy. Other than that, they are perfect.

One of the pluses of living in the 21st century is that we can take advantage of newly introduced plants while preserving past favourites. There are lots of vegetable varieties used in the past that we just don't grow any more, and Brittain loves the idea of reviving period plants that have slipped through the cracks of progress. Her passion stems from an environmental commitment to biodiversity (meaning a great variety of species). In 2000, she says, 90 percent of lettuce sold was iceberg lettuce. Heirloom vegetables have different genetic traits, and when they disappear, we lose those traits forever.

You don't have to choose between growing all heritage vegetables or all new hybrids because you can enjoy the benefits of both in a reasonably small garden. At the end of the day, I believe that diversity does make gardening infinitely more interesting—and better tasting, too.

*Macleans, Aug. 7, 2006

Locally Produced

"Wherever humans garden magnificently, there are magnificent heartbreaks."

–Henry Mitchell,
The Essential Earthman (1981)

CHAPTER 8

Man-made solutions abound at the garden centre. Until recent years, we took for granted that the only way to rid our lawn of weeds was to spray 2-4 D on them or, I suppose, dig them by hand. But 25 years' experience in the retail gardening business tells me that very few people indeed ever knelt down on the lawn and actually used a dandelion digger. (These do make great hose guides in the garden, though, if you shove them into the soil up to the handle.)

Now it is reasonably well known that you can rid your lawn of weeds quite nicely by competing them out of existence. Just spread some triple mix soil over the weedy area, rake smooth and spread quality grass seed over the triple mix. Water frequently and well until the new grass is established. Bingo. Weeds are gone and Bob's your uncle. (This works best in early spring and early September, by the way.)

Reaching for man-made solutions in the garden is well and good, but too often we overlook the solutions that Mother Nature has to offer. All we have to do is follow her example. Take shade gardening for instance. There are more plants that perform well in the shade than you can shake a shovel at. And many of them are "forest fresh," courtesy of your local growing conditions. Trilliums, Jack-in-the-pulpits, Canadian wild ginger, mayapple, countless ferns and many other native plants can help to create a beautiful shade garden in my area of Southern Ontario.

Wherever you live, I suggest that there's a similar lesson to be learned just by walking through the woods in your local area, especially in spring before the leaves are on the trees. I am not saying that you should go to your nearest woodlot and dig up the wildflowers—far from it. If you happen to know someone who owns one and you have their permission to remove a few plants, then you might try that—but be careful not to remove so many that you impact the local plant population. Instead, look for native plant species at your neighbourhood plant retailer and ask if they have been "nursery produced." That means that they haven't been stripped out of local habitat and that they will have a superior chance of establishing nicely in your garden.

The number of new plant nurseries that have sprouted up over recent years is amazing to me. Indeed, there is a native-owned nursery specializing in native plants on the Six Nations Reserve near Brantford, Ont. Linda and Ken Parker started their thriving enterprise growing sweet grass; thus, the name Sweet Grass Gardens. Look them up at www.sweetgrassgardens.com.

Caught up in our dreams and wish lists, we frequently overlook the obvious—such as local native plants—when planning our gardens. Keep in mind that Mother Nature has been very kind and generous to us, and we really need to pay attention to the valuable lessons she has to teach us.

The Golfer's Garden

"The gardener's foot does not spoil the garden."
—Italian saying

I have a woodland garden in my backyard. As I walk through it, I think of the many aspiring wildflower gardeners who are contemplating creating one of these natural beauties in their own yards.

A wildflower garden, be it a shady woodland or sunny meadow, is distinguished from other types of garden by the exclusive use of native plants. It is important that the plants you sow from seed and plant from transplants are truly native to your region and hardy in your growing zone.

Think of the word "wild" and you get a hint of how different this really is from our image of a traditional flower garden. If you're a traditional gardener who is just breaking into this thing we call native-plant gardening, you might be in for a bit of a shock. You see, one of the things that sets wildflower gardening apart is what you don't do. You don't rototill. You are very careful not to step on the flowers or the plants (that's why paths are so important). You pick the flowers infrequently and you definitely don't pick the seeds. Rather, you let the plants go to seed and self-propagate, allowing Mother Nature to do the work of filling in the blank spaces.

Finally, you generally do not apply synthetic fertilizers to a wildflower garden. Sometimes you don't even prepare the soil with generous quantities of compost or fresh top soil as I so often recommend with traditional gardens. Many wildflowers thrive in poor soil (I use the word "thrive" advisedly—they may struggle for a year or two, but if the species are chosen wisely in the first place, they will get used to it).

It is a very different process from that of planting a garden of nursery-cultivated trees, shrubs, evergreens and overgrown annual flowers. Native-plant gardening takes patience and a vision. Preferably, I might add, a vision that is flexible like a willow stick, because the ultimate picture will no doubt be different than the one you had in your head when you started.

Many of the flowering plants that you imagined would look spectacular will be dominated by other, more aggressive plant species. Unwanted plants (a.k.a. weeds) will try to establish themselves, providing lots of work for you in the form of hand-pulling them out. In the case of a wildflower meadow, you can mow the whole lot down twice a year (which prevents the weeds from going to seed and, as a bonus, adds nutrients to the soil). After a couple of years of this, you'll find the desired plants take hold. In time—count on at least three years—you will end up with the dense carpet of wildflowers that you wanted in the first place.

So, considering all the things that you don't do to maintain an established wildflower garden, what are you going to do with all the free time you're going to have? Well, that is the great fun of it—letting the garden "go to seed" while you find something else to occupy yourself with. Sounds like the perfect garden for the golfer.

A Tree on Loan

"He that plants trees loves others beside himself."

—Dr. Thomas Fuller,
Gnomologia (1732)

CHAPTER 10

I own a 1930 car. It is a fine thing to get in it on a sunny spring day and go for a drive. Every time that I do this, I think about the people who have driven my Model A over the years, the lives lived and the good times had on my set of four wheels. I think about the people who will drive it after me and the good times they will have.

If I take good care of my old car, chances are that it will last long enough for at least a couple more generations of drivers to enjoy it—which, to some degree, is the point of having a classic car in the first place. It is the succession of the thing. Classic car collectors amass cars not just to tinker with them and drive them but to preserve them.

When Mary and I bought our previous home, one that we lived in for 18 happy years, we chose the house on the basis of one thing—the towering forest of 16 mature hardwood trees that shrouded the home on the top of a hill. We had gorgeous sugar maples, white ash, an American elm and, the pièces de résistance, two giant red oaks that stood over 24 metres (80 feet) tall at the front of the house.

I loved those trees. I even talked with them.

One of our kids (Heather) enjoyed climbing them. And all of the family enjoyed the cool shade they produced each summer.

It is not a stretch to say that I believe each of those trees had a personality of its own. As Ralph Waldo Emerson said, in conversation with John Muir, "The wonder is that we can see these trees and not wonder more."

Consider how the role of a tree in your home landscape changes over time. On the day you plant it, you stand back and admire the spindly little item that you have just put in the ground. You spend the next five to 10 years pretty much ignoring it, just wishing that it would hurry up and grow up. You plant annuals around the base of it, perhaps, and carry on with other things. Meanwhile, the tree is busy producing roots and new growth all the while getting closer to your expectations for the shade and/or fruit that you expect it to provide.

In time, another homeowner moves in and sees the tree that you planted through very different eyes. When it is time to re-do the landscape (which occurs every 25 years or so), your tree has become the focal point, the real centrepiece around which the entire scheme for the garden is planned.

Notice that "your" tree now belongs to someone else. And there's the rub, my friend. The trees we plant are not ours—they are on loan to us. The real benefits of trees are enjoyed by future generations. In time, we do move on.

Perhaps that is the greatest tree-lesson of all. We plant them, nurture them, stake them and feed them only to have someone else enjoy the benefits of their maturity. It's kind of like having kids, don't you think?

The Purpose of a Hoe

*"Let your prayers for a good crop be short—
and your hoeing be long."*

—Albanian saying

CHAPTER 11

I thought I was the only one who looked at a hoe hanging in a garden shed the way I do. I thought that there couldn't possibly be anyone else who would attach such an extraordinary measure of importance to the weed-cutting tool that so many others take for granted.

But I found one such individual by the name of Jeff Taylor, who wrote the following in *Fine Gardening* magazine: "One could safely say that a hoe is the quintessential garden tool—and the same goes for the shovel, hand weeder, tiller, rake, etc. But only the hoe has serious words written in its honour, in [Edwin] Markham's 'The Man With the Hoe.' Although the poet equates this tool with brute labor, dead dreams, despair, and the loss of humanity to oppression, I suggest, instead, that a good hoe can connect spirit and body, sweat and psyche, mind and matter. It provides unbroken daydreaming time, thanks to the damnable tenacity of weeds." Before you ask what this is all about, let me explain on behalf of all hoe-lovers out there, of which there may be only two.

Take a warm sunny day, soft friable soil, a garden full of immature weeds that, though no more than three inches or so high, are quite prepared to take on the world, and your favourite, freshly sharpened hoe.

You now have a recipe for an existential experience.

Start at one end of the garden and begin to mow down the weeds by pulling the hoe back towards you, barely stroking the surface of the soil. Take another stroke and another until you develop a rhythm.

Take your time with this. Keep going until you are no longer thinking about the hoeing. Let the clean air, birdsong and vision of the perfect weed-free garden fill your head. Take more time. Don't rush and don't strain your shoulders (that is where the sharp hoe is key). And be sure to leave the portable phone, pager and any other listening device that you may stick into your ear in the house.

This is your break. It is your diversion from the noise of life that so often obstructs otherwise creative thoughts and day-dreams.

You are now getting it.

What is the purpose of a hoe?

Put in context, it is the perfect dream-weaver. Don't judge us until you have experienced it. Jeff and I rest our case.

Sky-High Gardening

CHAPTER 12

*"Gardens are not made by singing 'Oh, how beautiful!'
and sitting in the shade."*
—Rudyard Kipling

The other day I attended a thought-provoking seminar on green roofs. Now, I have long known that the black tar traditionally used to waterproof flat roofs makes absolutely no sense at all. Solar heat is attracted to black tar, which sucks it up like sponge cake and radiates it into the dwelling below. Then the biggest air-conditioning unit that the rafters can hold is plunked on the same roof to push cooled air down into the same living space below at great expense to the wallet and the environment.

Along come some logical thinking scientists who know a couple of things about how the world works. They know, for instance, that all the oxygen we breathe is manufactured by green, living plants; that hot air rises and cool air falls; and that engineers of roofs for the past century or so are basically lazy or they would have figured this one out by now. Take these complementary thoughts and put them on a flat roof in the form of a low-growing garden and you have a brilliant idea.

In London, England, the highest green roof in Europe has now been completed with fully established wind- and drought-tolerant plants. Created 152 metres (500 feet) above the ground (about 50 storeys high), it covers 409 square metres (4,400 square feet) on the top of Barclays Bank headquarters at Canary Wharf.

At first, it was thought that this could not be done at this height, that no plants would survive up there and that no wildlife would find it anyway.

Wrong-o.

Some of the U.K.'s rarest breeding birds, black redstarts, have already been sighted on the roof as have ladybugs and grasshoppers. (Grasshoppers? I haven't seen a grasshopper fly more than about 15 feet in my yard.)

The designers really thought this through; mixing locally sourced crushed brick and concrete with small amounts of soil pre-seeded with a wildflower mix. They even created an arid, exposed environment to attract certain insects by including some circular areas of pebbles. Evidently this is a good place to mate, if you are a certain insect.

Now they have a cooler roof and a building that uses less energy to heat and to cool. They have a sky-high garden that includes some interesting wildflower species and provides habitat for local wildlife. The green roof absorbs rain and uses it to the benefit of the sedums, ornamental grasses and other plants that are at home up there—that means less water going into the already strained London stormwater drains.

The downside—what downside?

The only downside is that I didn't think of it.

Mother Nature Has a Better Idea

"Nature's first green is gold. Her hardest hue to hold."
—Robert Frost,
"Nothing Gold Can Stay"

CHAPTER 13

Inspiration comes from some of the strangest—and often the most obvious—places. Many of my ideas for garden designs come from the natural areas that surround our country home, from the tapestry of plants under the woodland's canopy of shade to the hot hues of sunny borders. If you look closely, you'll see that Mother Nature has the ability to combine plant material and colours in the most brilliant ways. Then she illuminates them with natural sunlight, the best possible light for comparing colours.

My wife, Mary, is a passionate knitter and often takes handfuls of knitting yarn to the window to study how the different tints look together. She will mix and match them until she finds a combination that works. The sun beaming in through a south- or west-facing window tells the truth where colour is concerned. Most of our man-made light distorts true colours.

Interior designers often look to the outdoors for colour inspiration. Visit any hardware store and peruse the paint department. You will likely find pictures of plants and gardens used to create colour "themes" in their selection. It's an attempt to bring to life the paint that you'll use inside because nothing looks more real than nature's own.

"Painting" with flowers in the garden is a lot of the fun.

Take your time to look over the colours in your borders. Sometimes seedlings you never planted (called volunteers) pop up in the most surprising places, creating colour combinations you may never have thought of (but can take credit for).

How many of us have walked around the garden, a new plant in hand, looking for the perfect companion for it? Here is a little tip to help the confounded colour-matcher. Go outside and pick a flower, say a pansy. Any pansy will do. Take a good look at it, peer right into the centre. See how many colours are actually in the heart of the bloom-cream, a hint of orange and almost always, a spot of yellow. That tiny spot of bright yellow sets off the other colours that make up 98 percent of the rest of the pansy. And if you put the pansy with other yellow flowers, your eye will actually pick up the echo of yellow in the pansies. You can do this with other flowers, too, like daylilies and irises, so you can always have colour combinations that work.

There you have it—a nifty shortcut that garden designers use all the time. And provided free of charge by Mother Nature.

Remember When
We Dreamed About Sex?

*"A woman complained that her roses were too tall for her
to reach the flowers. 'Give it an occasional prune,' I said.
Several weeks later, the woman called up and said,
'It's had half a tin of prunes now,
and it still doesn't seem to be improving.'"*

—Alan Titchmarsh,
British garden writer

A couple of years ago, on the coldest night of the winter, I found myself in the woods in a cabin filled with about 27 little guys in Wolf Cub uniforms. And about four other grown men in Wolf Cub Leader uniforms. We had enjoyed a full day of frolicking about in the great Canadian snow: cross-country skiing, snowshoeing, playing snow tag and snow tetherball, etc. By nighttime, we were tired and well-fed, and the air in the cabin hung with an odour that would not make any mother proud. We were exhausted and finally it came time for bed.

Perhaps that is why I had the most wonderful dream that night (an effort to escape the reality of my situation, do you suppose?). While I seldom remember my dreams—or make the effort to—I remember this one as vividly as if it happened last night.

I dreamt that I was leaving the house for work, briefcase in hand, wearing a sweater and appropriate business attire. I opened the door and there in our front yard was the most extraordinary exhibit of colour, something not seen since the previous summer. My garden was in full bloom! I could hear the hum of busy bumblebees, see butterflies on the wing, and of course the roses and container plants that I normally grow outside my front door looked spectacular. I stood there speechless.

My wife, Mary, who had walked to the door with me, looked out at the summer garden bathed in sunlight and said, "I think you should stay home today and work in the garden. We don't get too many days like this," (an understatement in mid-January, to say the least). I agreed with her. I dreamt that I ran upstairs, changed into my jeans, stayed home and that is the end of the story. Except that I woke up.

I was sleeping on the bottom bunk and there was a loud thud from the top where another guy named Mark (a bigger model than me) was making his way down the ladder in his famous red, all-wool, one-piece, long underwear (the kind you saw as a kid in your Christmas reader, the one with "The Night Before Christmas" in it).

I was so excited by my awesome dream that I had to tell big Mark about it. In detail, I talked about the colour, the butterflies, the bees and he looked at me patiently. As he listened, a grin began creeping across his face until I finally finished. Then he said, "You really dreamed that. About gardening?" His tone was incredulous.

"Well, yes!" I exclaimed. And he replied, "Do you even remember when we dreamed about sex?"

I didn't bother telling the story to anyone else.

An Environmental Cure-All

*"Thanksgiving was never meant
to be shut up in a single day."*
–Robert Casper Linter

T he people responsible for meeting the international obligations of the Kyoto Accord seem determined to make things very complicated.

Evidently, countries that signed on to the accord are using a formula to calculate the amount of carbon dioxide produced by a nation; there are debits and credits depending on how much pollution a given population produces. If your country has lots of money, you can actually buy the credits that have been generated by another country.

Now don't get me wrong. I am in favour of anything that helps to prolong the life of good old Mother Earth, but I have another idea. How about we require everyone with access to a piece of real estate—no matter how small—to plant trees? The number and size of the trees you would be required to plant would depend on the size of your real estate. If you live in a townhouse or, for that matter, an apartment or high-rise condo, you would plant deciduous shrubs in containers.

Here are the facts that make this such a fabulous idea: Trees help to keep global temperatures under control since they use and store carbon dioxide as they grow. Trees can reduce temperatures as much as nine degrees during the summer. A mature tree removes 11.8 kg (26 pounds) of carbon dioxide from the air each year and releases about 5.9 kg (13 pounds) of oxygen each day. This is enough oxygen to sustain a family of four. A well-located, large deciduous tree can reduce air-conditioning costs by 10 to 50 percent or, put another way, can save you several hundred dollars a year. One tree will filter air-borne pollutants for 25 to 100 years or more, demanding no more than a drink of water from time to time and some space to stretch out its roots (though I am always shocked how little soil is required to grow many street trees successfully).

In addition, trees prevent erosion, control stormwater runoff, and provide food and shelter for wildlife (including neighbourhood squirrels, but hey, this is not a panacea).

When I think about it, the trees in our neighbourhood are living, growing clean-air machines that only quit long after we have done the planting.

I am not against other alternatives—hybrid cars, wind-generated electrical power, even nuclear power (if only someone could figure out where to put the waste when we are through with it)—but if we all planted more trees and drove around a little less, imagine the impact!

And think of the nice things that our grandchildren would be saying about us. The alternative is to continue to run amok with what we have inherited, environmentally speaking. And be bad-mouthed for generations to come.

Putting an End to Bad Jokes

"What sunshine is to flowers, smiles are to humanity....Scattered along life's pathway, the good they do is inconceivable."

—Joseph Addison

You have heard them, I have heard them and we've had about enough. Bad jokes. Or maybe good jokes you have heard so many times that they are no longer funny. Think how many characters have shared this bit of gardening lore: "I fed my lawn a shot of Scotch and it came up half cut." I think I might have laughed the first time.

Now along comes a report based on real experience that might just give credence to the Scotch joke. Seems that Bill Miller of the Flower Bulb Research Program at Cornell University in Ithaca, New York, has tested the theory that a little bit of alcohol can actually make plants grow shorter.*

The test plants were paperwhites, those white or yellow narcissus that you pot up in the fall to bloom indoors in winter. Miller used a water solution containing four to six percent alcohol (any hard liquor will do but not beer or wine because they contain too much sugar; suits me because I am not a fan of hard liquor though I love the odd beer. I even love the even ones).

To get a five percent solution using a 40 percent distilled spirit such as gin or vodka, you need to add one part liquor to seven parts water. You could also use rubbing alcohol, but since

that is usually 70 percent alcohol, you should make the
dilution with one part rubbing alcohol to 10 or 11 parts water.
(This would be much cheaper than the other alcohol sources
mentioned, but your friends will be less impressed with your
story.)

Once the shoots of the paperwhites are 2.5 to five cm
(one to two inches) tall, start using this solution to water them.
The plants will be about one-third shorter but the flowers are
unaffected, so you get the bloom you want without floppy
plants. No staking, no falling over onto the floor for the cat to
play with. So could watering your lawn with alcohol actually
cause it to grow shorter? I don't have the budget to try it on my
lawn, but if you would like to be the guinea pig, please go for it
and let me know how you do.

By the way, Miller says that they saw growth problems
start when they went to about 10 percent alcohol, and that
25 percent alcohol proved to be dramatically toxic.

This proves another thing—something that I have been
saying for years..Plants are people too.

No kidding.

*Green Profit Magazine, June, 2006

Apples as the Next Green Fuel

"Gardener's gold, I load and pile it
Mix it, turn it, wait and while it
Cooks I test it every smelly couple of days:
Plunge my hand into the steaming
Reeking middle, what's it needing...
Air? or water? 'One more week.' The odour says."

—Thea Gavin,
"Ode to a Road Apple"

CHAPTER 17

For some time I have been thinking that our 20 hectares (50 acres) would be the perfect place to create a "wind farm." I would just put up 20 or 30 big windmills, get the bank to pay for them and I would sit back and collect big cheques each month from the local utility while my brother-in-law continues to sweat it out in the fields growing soybeans and deking around the windmills. I would pay a little interest to the bank for the loan and never have to worry that we might run out of power, at least not on windy days. And Lord knows with the wonderful western exposure we enjoy, we have big-time wind!

On the topic of environmentally-friendly wacky ideas, there is a group that is way ahead of me. According to the British magazine, *The Garden*, the future of many famous Herefordshire cider orchards could be secured if an unusual project to turn apples into "green" electricity gets off the ground. Recently, a company called Coressence was formed with the intent of converting the estimated 36,000 metric tons (40,000 tons) of excess cider apples produced yearly into pure alcohol (bioethanol, to be exact). This alcohol is then burned in a gas-turbine heat-and-power unit, with the resulting electricity exported to the grid.

Not only could this supply Hereford with seven percent of its electricity needs but it could also keep some 400 orchard businesses afloat and save about 360,000 oxygen-producing trees from being cut down. Employment in the area would remain stable and maybe improve. And the apple-mash would make fabulous compost, so all the local gardeners would be very happy.

The excess fruit has come about because of declining demand for cider and the ending of contracts between growers and cider-makers. As this is the main outlet for the fruit, the Herefordshire Sustain Project's Orchard Topic Group set about finding alternative uses. Its first idea of using the fruits' bioethanol in the production of biodiesel proved to be uneconomical, but turning the alcohol into electricity is financially feasible because it is deemed renewable and thus attracts a subsidy.

Coressence's Katie Eastaugh says: "We believe it can happen; it is just a case of how quickly."* The firm is looking at partnerships with a local college and consultants to source or design the machinery needed for bioethanol production. It could also be good news for organic orchards planted with old or local cultivars: because fruit for electricity conversion does not have to look good to consumers, it can be grown without chemicals. So keep this in mind, "Today's wacky idea is tomorrow's reality."

*The Garden, October, 2005 .

The Monk Tree

"Speak to me from your heart, and I'll listen with mine."
—Peter de Jager

People who know me best know that my first love where gardening is concerned is trees. I connect with some; I admire them all. In my opinion, we can learn a lot from trees and their history.

The ginkgo tree was thought to be extinct until a visitor to an ancient Buddhist monastery in the heart of China "discovered" several specimens growing in the courtyard there—old trees, living fossils actually, with a pedigree that reaches back millions of years in a religious place that had stood for a relatively short thousand years or so.

Trees, you see, can put life into perspective by their very existence. Their age and perseverance tells us a lot about their nature; their growth habits and bark can tell us a lot about their history.

I believe that trees talk to those of us willing to listen. I don't mean that you need to put your ear to the bark of a tree hoping that it might say something—although you might try this and have more success than I have. Trees talk to us when we listen with our eyes. Take the "monk birch" that I pass every time I travel from downtown Toronto to my home north of the city. As you leave the city and go up the Don Valley Parkway, you very soon pass by an island of grass that sits between the two streams of ceaseless traffic. The island is there to provide space for a hydro tower that keeps the electrical wires in the air. And standing directly under the tower is a 7.6-metre (25-foot) birch. It has been there much longer than you might expect for a tree of its size. I know; I have been watching it for years and it never seems to get any bigger. How could it, sucking in all that pollution from the thousands of vehicles that course by it every day?

I call it the "monk birch" because it bends over the pavement oh so slightly and hangs there, as if giving its blessing to every traveller that passes beneath it. What is the monk birch saying to me as I drive along at 120 kilometres an hour? Sometimes it says, "Take it easy, slow down," sometimes "Go safe," and sometimes "Remember your destination" (like home to see your family!).

I can count on this tree to be there for me every time I go up the highway.

That I can count on it to be there at all may be lesson enough for an old tree.

Perennial Lovers

"Of all human activities,
apart from procreation of children,
gardening is the most optimistic and hopeful."
—Susan Hill

Barbara Frum, the late Canadian broadcast journalist, was widely acclaimed for her many gifts in the field of mass communication; she was also a passionate gardener. It was Frum who said, "Gardening is fundamentally an act of enormous hope, because everything that you do in the garden is for the future."

In a recent column in the *Globe and Mail*, food critic (and gardener) Joanne Kates expressed her opinion of our favourite leisure-time activity. Her response to the question, why is gardening growing in popularity, was this: "Hope is in insufficient supply these days."

I strongly believe that the experience of gardening (as opposed to the mere observation of gardens) settles us down and allows us to luxuriate in the future, while benefiting from the exercise of today. The activity of gardening, whether you are digging, planting, seed-sowing or weeding, is grounded in the future and thus, is an act of optimism.

Kates puts it this way, "Who are perennial gardeners if not the greatest optimists in the world, to believe that not only will a wonderful renaissance actually happen, but also that we'll be there to witness it? Who needs other enchantments when you have a garden to tend?"

Well, there are some other enchantments that I enjoy besides my garden. There are times in the spring and fall when a ride through the countryside in my convertible, with the top down of course, is enchanting. Similarly, taking out my 1930 Ford Model A can be delightful in a nostalgic way. I love to drive down quiet roads and imagine who drove this car before me and how liberating the feeling must have been for those whose alternative mode of transport was a horse. But those other enchantments seem superficial compared to that of my garden. That is something that grows with you, and you with it, through the seasons and through the years.

As Kates writes so eloquently, "The garden in fall resembles my middle age. Bloom there is a plenty, but it is not the riot of fresh exuberant colour of spring or summer. My fall garden is a quieter symphony: dusty-rose sedums, tall, dark-purple monkshood, pale gold and grey-green grasses that sway and rustle in every breeze, perennial hibiscus in the lavender palette, hydrangeas in pink. We have a certain sympathy, my garden and I, for neither of us is in the first bloom of our youth, and yet there is pleasure in this season, perhaps the sweeter for knowing that nothing goes on forever."*

Name your season and from where I kneel, I will show you countless good reasons why the garden moves us forward, using its own language to offer us beauty and hope.

*Globe and Mail, Sept. 29, 2006.

Lessons Learned From Cottagers

"Everything that slows us down and forces patience, everything that sets us back into the slow circles of nature, is a help."

—May Sarton

I have never been a cottager, never wanted to be one. Certainly on a Friday afternoon in summer from the comfort of my own yard, I am pleased not to count myself among the gifted folk who battle the traffic heading north to the lake country.

I seem to have spent a lot of time over the past 25 years or so defending my position on the subject. There are a lot of cottagers who are very passionate about their oasis in the mosquito-infested woods (oh, sorry, my prejudice just slipped out there) and seem to think that everyone would be happier up there.

Of late, however, I've been thinking that the weekend experience at the cottage has its pluses, and that we gardeners could probably learn something from cottagers. It has to do with the expression, "Stop and smell the roses."

It's a popular activity in cottage country to get up early, take a cup of coffee out to the dock and listen to the silence, broken occasionally by the cry of a loon or the odd fish jumping. The morning mist on the quiet of the lake creates mystery and enchantment.

You might as well enjoy this unusual early-morning environment as you sure aren't likely to find a morning newspaper for miles.

All kidding aside, the truth is that cottagers are much better than us gardeners at slowing down and drinking in the sights and sounds of Mother Nature.

Many gardeners don't stop long enough to see what lies beyond the toil and sweat of the gardening experience because we love it so, sometimes to the point of obsession. I can certainly be one of those people, which is perhaps why my kids call me the Energizer Bunny. But we need to relax once in a while, like our cottaging brethren.

When sanity finally prevails, I like to lie in the hammock, close to a tree where I can give myself a push. The rocking motion of the hammock is perfect for daydreaming and listening to the garden.

Try this—having set yourself up, shut your eyes and open your ears. Don't just stop and smell the roses; listen to the roses. And the buzzing of the bees or, if you're lucky enough, maybe a hummingbird, or the breeze rustling the leaves of your trees, or water trickling somewhere in your garden.

I'll take a page out of the "book according to cottagers" and from time to time, leave home behind as well as the phone, fax, Blackberry and pager. I like to do this without the commute.

It's time to dream. Right here in my garden.

Better Than Money in the Bank

"Things that I remember: witnessing childbirth.
Finding myself standing absolutely alone before
Da Vinci's Last Supper. And planting potatoes
on a perfect spring morning."

–William Alexander,
The $64 Tomato

I read in a financial magazine recently that people spend more time planting their bedding plants than they do planning their financial future. The article made it sound as if this was newsworthy information—shocking, in fact.

Well, excuse me, but I thought that's what professional financial planners were for. As a consumer of financial planning services, I ask you, did your "wealth management professional" go to school to earn their certification, spend all that money on an office, equipment and staff just so they could burden you with the details of planning your financial future? Did they ask those endless questions at your first meeting because they are just nosey?

I'll be the first to admit that I spend a whole lot more time planting annuals than I do planning my financial future. I might even add that I spend more time watching the Toronto Maple Leafs make fools of themselves (though they seem to be doing quite well at the moment, but I digress) than I do financial planning.

Since when did planning your financial future provide all the benefits that gardening does? Does poring over spreadsheets bring families together like the activity of planning, planting and nurturing the garden? Or growing fresh fruit and vegetables? I know people who will boast about their tomato crop or the size of their pumpkins with more zest and enthusiasm than anyone who made a bundle on the stock market. Sure, the money can be good, but the satisfaction is as fleeting as the next stock market dip. Besides, apart from making a well-timed decision, what did the investor actually do, other than take a risk?

I don't know who said that the best bet you can make is with some good soil and a packet of seeds, but he or she had a point. The risks are few and the potential rewards many.

In gardening, we engage in a partnership with Mother Nature and grow relationships with neighbours and friends, creating a sense of community that is without price. I believe that people who spend time writing for the financial pages and the financial planners themselves would actually benefit by spending more time in the garden.

The healthy diversions of gardening provide the very best therapy for people who work under a lot of pressure, offering high returns for a small investment of effort.

And you can take that to the bank.

Garden Grunts

*"All the wars of the world, all the Caesars,
have not the staying power of a lily in a cottage garden."*

—Reginald Farrer,
The Rainbow Bridge (1921)

CHAPTER 22

I was looking for a hosta variety that would perform around the base of an old sugar maple in my front yard. I saw in my mind's eye this beautiful show of variegated foliage, punctuated with soft lavender blossoms in midsummer. I wanted a mass planting of 25 or 30 hostas of the same variety to create real impact as people drove by our house.

I consulted my friend and professional nursery farmer Carolyn Hardie. She has been growing perennials for years and really knows her stuff.

"Carolyn, I need a hosta that is really tough—able to withstand the competition of the mature tree roots and the lack of water around my maple and resilient enough to put on a show."

"Oh," said Carolyn, "you need a hosta with grunt." Without hesitation, she recommended *Hosta* 'Sagae'.

She was right. I took 27 plants of 'Sagae' home and found that the roots were so aggressive I had to cut the pots off with a sharp knife. As I planted them, I thought about Carolyn's description, and other plants with grunt: tough perennial customers that take root quickly and get going, bloom their heads off and never quit. Purebred competitors, they are good friends to the low-maintenance gardener.

I thought of purple coneflower (*Echinacea purpurea*) for one, and *Scabiosa* 'Butterfly Blue', which is known to produce flowers even after the first snowfall. The new hybrid pansies and violas are plants with grunt. They not only don't quit, but they also seed themselves and multiply like crazy.

However, plants such as goutweed (*Aegopodium podagraria*) and mint misbehave too much to qualify as garden grunts. They just don't seem to understand their rightful place.

There are gardeners with grunt, too.

You see them outdoors in early spring before the frost is out of the ground. They are turning their compost, hardening off seedlings by day, planting up their dahlia tubers by night. In autumn they fertilize their lawn in November, just as the books tell us to. They winterize their roses with rose collars, and you can spot them out there in the rain raking the leaves off the lawn.

They are garden champions who defy the elements to get the job done. Get to know them and you will realize that they actually love these challenges.

Well, "challenges" to normal people, "opportunities" to them. God bless them all. We could use more garden grunts.

Plant Signs and Symbols

"Spread the feeling of generosity,
using plants between stepping stones."
—Gordon Hayward

The more I learn about the history of humankind, the more fascinated I become with the stories about plants that are woven into that history. For instance, according to a popular tale in British Columbia, native people carried around a single acorn from an oak as a way of symbolizing eternal youth.

Many plants have historical connections and meaning: in Victorian times, the red rose came to signify passion and love, and the white chrysanthemum represented truth. Plants have become national symbols: Canada has the sugar maple leaf; Scotland, the thistle; Holland, the tulip; and Ireland, the four-leafed clover. And of course there are universal symbols such as the olive branch signifying peace.

Speaking of peace, one of my favourite stories of all is that of Francis Meilland, the famous rose grower in France who grew a glorious hybrid tea rose with no name. He knew it was a winner, but in 1939, he received word that the Nazis were marching across the country, about to shut down any contact with the outside.

Quickly, he bundled up cuttings of his treasured new rose and sent them to his friend Robert Pyle at the Conard-Pyle Nursery in Pennsylvania. Years went by without communication until 1945 and the war's end, when Meilland re-connected with his good friend in the States. Standing in the massive rose-growing fields of the Conard-Pyle Nursery, the two men knew this rose had great potential, so they entered it into the All-American Rose Selections, the Academy Awards of the rose world.

They won.

Later in 1945, the United Nations was being formed and to commemorate the inaugural meeting, delegates were given the new rose with creamy white petals edged in delicate carmine that had originated in recently liberated France.

The name of the rose? Why, 'Peace', of course.

And over the following six decades, that rose has gone on to become one of the most popular garden roses in the world.

Not All Plants Are Created Equal

CHAPTER 24

"There is enough misery in the world without thinking about Norway maples."

—Henry Mitchell,
The Essential Earthman (1981)

From time to time, I am asked what I think of weeping willows. How do you respond to a question like that, when you know the person asking either wants you to say something nice because they like the plant, or is secretly setting you up to settle a domestic dispute (i.e. he hates it/she loves it)?

As in all things (well, most things), I do as my dad taught me and tell the truth. I hate weeping willows.

Maybe it goes back to the days when I was in my teens, cutting my teeth in the business for $1.25 an hour at my dad's garden centre. The surrounding neighbourhood was rife with Lombardy poplars and weeping willows. Know why? Because the original homeowners were too impatient to wait for quality trees to mature.

As a result, my generation inherited neighbourhoods that were generally devoid of any permanent beauty in the landscape. By the time I was serving the gardening public, those rampantly growing softwood trees were coming down at a furious pace. The ones that didn't blow down were cut down to avoid the hazard. And in their place the number-one recommendation was the Norway maple.

Yes, I enjoyed selling the Norway, with its lovely fall colour, symmetrical crown, relative fast growth habit, tolerance of polluted city air, and good-natured willingness to accept the rigours of transplanting without dying. Indeed, my dad made lots of money growing and selling Norways.

Today, *Acer platanoides* appears on any self-respecting list of noxious weeds. Naturalists, environmentalists and tree-hugging purists alike are on a campaign to cut down and replace the Norway maple with something better behaved that does not reproduce so vigorously or invade our natural woodlands to the detriment of native species.

I cannot blame them. I'm on the bandwagon too, as hypocritical as that may seem. My excuse for being so thoughtless is borrowed from the book of How to Succeed in Politics 101 — I didn't know better at the time.

The native sugar maple (*Acer saccharum*) is now the principal recommended replacement for the Norway. When I was working for my dad, we said that the sugar maple was ideal for use in the country but was a poor urban tree as it was not very resistant to acid rain and pollution. We sold very few of them. What changed? Tree breeders developed new varieties of sugar maple that have proved to be quite adaptable to city conditions.

Over the years, the business of gardening has altered — we have become smarter and now know better than to recommend aggressive plants for the garden. Today we look at our gardening activity in a much more holistic way, with a view to the impact we have on our broader environment, not just our piece of real estate.

As for the weeping willow, I recommend it in a country setting, planted by the edge of a pond, at least 150 metres (500 feet) away from any underground wires or pipes and in a place where it can shed all the twigs and junk it likes, providing that the owner doesn't mind going out and picking up after it every time a wind comes up.

Given all that, it is a great tree.

There is a growing pool of knowledge regarding gardening and the environment—all the more reason to remain open-minded and to keep reading and listening for new information that will make us better gardeners and citizens. Perhaps like the willow, we need to be flexible and bend our opinions from time to time.

How to Feel More Compassionate and Happier

"There is material enough in a single flower for the ornament of a score of cathedrals."

—John Ruskin,
The Stones of Venice (1851)

As a guy, I could be accused of being in that elite group of people who are a little less sensitive than the other half of the people who inhabit the planet. So forgive me if what I am about to tell you is not news to you.

Researchers at Harvard University have recently shown that people feel more compassionate toward others, have less worry and anxiety, and feel less depressed when flowers are present in the home or office.

The Home Ecology of Flowers Study is the result of a partnership between the Society of American Florists (SAF), the Flower Promotion Organization (FPO), and psychologist Nancy Etcoff, Ph.D., of Massachusetts General Hospital and Harvard Medical School (HMS)—enough acronyms for you?

Here are a few of the highlights from the research:
· Study participants who lived with flowers for less than a week felt an increase in feelings of compassion for others.
· Participants felt less negative after being around flowers at home for just a few days.
· People are more likely to feel happier and have more enthusiasm and energy at work when flowers are in their environment.

CHAPTER 25

Dr. Etcoff said, "As a psychologist, I'm particularly intrigued to find that people who live with flowers report fewer episodes of anxiety and depressed feelings. In all, our results suggest that flowers have a positive impact on well-being."*

Not to take anything away from the good doctor's observations, but I think she is downplaying the most important point. As an employer, I am most intrigued to find that people feel happier and have more enthusiasm and energy at work when flowers are around them.

This has given me a great idea. As an employer who is always interested in the welfare of my people, I am going to put fresh flowers in my next quarterly budget. They will be delivered fresh to the office directly to each employee on a weekly basis. If employees want to take the arrangements home at the end of each week, they can do that and feel even better there, too.

Given this new proof that flowers are really good for people and that flowers improve workers' productivity, don't you think it is a great idea to put flowers in all work places?

And who was that who accused me of lacking sensitivity?

*GrowerTalks, November, 2006

Glow-in-the-Dark Love

"Correct handling of flowers refines the personality."
—Gustie L. Herrigel,
Zen in the Art of Flower Arrangement (1958)

CHAPTER 26

Here is a revolutionary concept that will give new meaning to the old slogan, "Say it with flowers." Glow-in-the-dark roses and chrysanthemums. Yes, they actually "light up" in the dark. Marketed as Glowing Flowers, the flowers are treated with a dye and are then exposed to daylight or black light to "charge" them. Plants look normal under natural light conditions, but then glow in the dark rather eerily for several hours.

Apparently, the treatment doesn't affect the life span of the blooms. This "bright" idea is the invention of Frank de Koning, whose company De Koning BV has the exclusive right to use the patented dye on ornamental flowers and plants. His initial offerings, the roses and chrysanthemums, were brought to market by the FloraHolland auction in Naadlwijk, the Netherlands, according to *GrowerTalks* magazine.

Now, all this is very exciting, but I have a few questions: As an organic gardener, can I purchase these flowers and give them to someone knowing that I am not offending the principles for which I stand? Is the environment going to thank me for buying this product, given the process that they have gone through? I confess I am just a little suspicious of a treatment that calls for the spraying of a dye that absorbs light.

Here is a really stupid question, but one that we need to

think about before we run out and pay a premium (no doubt) for these charged-up flowers. When putting the finished flowers in my compost, is the compost pile going to glow in the dark, too?

All the better for the raccoons to find it, I guess. I need to think this through a little bit before I jump on the bandwagon of plugged-in colour.

Finally, and what is really on my mind, is this question: If flowers are the language of love, then why illuminate the room when the lights go out?

I am in favour of letting the old-fashioned flowers that I can't see in the dark work their magic. History tells me that this works just fine.

Love Your Garden, Worts and All

> *"If one were as good a gardener in practice as one is
> in theory, what a garden would one create!"*
>
> —**Vita Sackville-West,**
> *Some Flowers* (1937)

CHAPTER 27

If you love to garden and have learned both the common and botanical names of plants, you are well on your way to knowing a whole lot more about the historic uses and myths attached to them. Take the many "worts" in your garden, including leadwort (*Ceratostigma plumbaginoides*), madwort (*Alyssum*), liverwort (*Hepatica*) and lungwort (*Pulmonaria*).

The word "wort" comes from the Anglo-Saxon *wyrt,* simply meaning "plant." According to Lyn Tremblay, a writer for *Ontario Gardener,* most worts are herbs that were cultivated for their medicinal qualities as described in folklore or touted by ancient herbalists.

The prefix to "wort" gives additional clues. For instance, lungwort was used to treat patients with lung problems and complaints of the chest. Our forebears believed in the doctrine of signatures—i.e., that a plant's appearance determined its purpose—and thought the blotchy leaves of *Pulmonaria* resembled lungs.

Liverwort, one of our earliest blooming wildflowers, has leaves the shape and colour of a liver, so it was thought to be effective in treating that organ.

Leadwort, a popular ground cover in zones 5 to 9, provides us with some gorgeous blue flowers in early fall, followed by maroon-red leaves. It was commonly believed that this plant would cure lead poisoning. After someone had taken a lead bullet under the skin, you wonder how much help the leadwort would have been; however, maybe they had their ways.

And if leadwort really did help to treat lead poisoning, perhaps the ancient Romans could have used it to their benefit after the entire population was poisoned by the water that ran through lead pipes in urban areas. It might have saved the empire. Imagine how differently our world would have turned out. All because of a plant.

Madwort, oddly enough, is better known by its botanical name—*Alyssum*. This sweet-smelling annual in frothy white or purple are very popular in spring. It is also known for self-seeding everywhere. At one time, it was thought that this plant cured madness or could help cure rabies, contracted when one was bitten by a mad dog or other carrier.

When you learn the names of the plants in your garden, you are not only learning a new language, you are also logging into your hard drive a new understanding of people-plant connections.

Both common and botanical names can indicate not only the plant's use but also its origin, growth habit, a physical characteristic or its preferred growing conditions. All this is interesting to know and useful when siting plants in our gardens. All you might have to do is look up the meaning of the botanical words (usually Latin or Greek).

There are many excellent books on plant nomenclature. If you search the web or your local library, you will likely find a few. My favourite is my treasured *Henderson's Handbook of Plants*, published by Peter Henderson and Co. in 1881.

Given its age, you can see why I treasure it, like the many worts in my garden.

We Have Work to Do!

"To be good is noble; but to show others how to be good is nobler and no trouble."

—Mark Twain

I almost never use the word "work" in association with gardening. It is my heartfelt belief that the two words have nothing in common.

Gardening should be associated with sweet smells, glorious sights, feelings of satisfaction and downright delight—whether you are involved in a garden activity or just sitting in a garden with a cold drink in your hand, taking it all in. Work is about working. You don't do that in the garden unless you would rather be somewhere else, like on the golf course. Which is a whole other story.

As gardeners, we have our work cut out for us just the same. Let me illustrate.

I belong to a group that is loosely organized around the theme of family business. The 10 of us meet every couple of months for a few hours to talk and exchange ideas. We always use a question that each of us is required to answer as an ice-breaker. On one occasion, the question was, "If you were given one week to enjoy the experience of the northern wilderness, what would you do with it?"

Most of us responded by waxing on romantically about paddling a canoe with someone we love (a spouse was a popular theme), enjoying the fresh air and the silence of the north.

One guy, we will call him Terrie, said he would enjoy teaching his kids (all four of them) to fish. That way he would not have to keep feeding them with expensive store-bought food. (It's a shame the way some people spoil a good idea with too much information.)

Another, we'll call him Timm, said he would cut down the forest for lumber, blast the rock for road-building and siphon the fresh-water springs for bottling (yes, there is likely money in that—what an original idea).

This drew the predictable response of laughter and hilarity from the group. I would have considered it very funny, too, had I thought he was kidding.

Truth is, Timm is in the road-building business up north. While he may have been kidding with this one, he makes his living doing precisely that—cutting, blasting and moving water out of the way.

Now, I understand the need for people to make a living, within the bounds of existing laws, any way they choose. And I believe that Timm actually values his northern experience. He loves his cottage, after all.

However, we live in two universes—one that gives us the comfort and the safety of a controlled "man-made" environment and the other is a world of love and respect for the planet and what's left of it.

Gardeners tend to live more in the latter universe: doing what we can to enhance our small corner of the planet and make it better. We also have a responsibility to remind people that this is not our planet alone, but one that we share. Gardening is just one method of improving the quality of Mother Earth, and one of very few that actually can provide us with comfort and safety without doing harm.

Getting the message out, however, can be a lot of work, and getting through to some people is more work than to others.

Small "O" Organic Gardener

"Who would look dangerously up at Planets
that might safely look downe at Plants?"

—John Gerrard,
Herball or Generall Historie of Plantes (1597)

CHAPTER 29

When you live in a free country like Canada, there should be no need to defend what you do, providing you aren't breaking any laws. So when I say that I am an organic gardener, I shouldn't have to explain why.

The 25 years that I have spent writing and broadcasting about gardening—the 17 books, and hundreds of articles and TV and radio shows—have been based on my belief that we can garden successfully without the use of synthetic pesticides, pretty much.

My explanation and a little history:

I was brought up in the gardening business. My father Len ran several retail garden centres and had no qualms about selling nicotine sulphate, Malathion, Cygon 2E and even DDT (before my time). Applying these chemicals to your garden was the accepted way to solve a host of gardening problems, with very little thought given to the problems created in the process. Mercifully, all the above-mentioned chemicals are now off the Canadian market.

And we have taken some time to think through the effects of using toxic chemicals in the garden.

I began thinking about it seriously when our firstborn arrived 24 years ago. I took at look at baby Lynn and then at the arsenal in my toolshed and garage and realized that there was something missing in my logic: new baby on the one hand and containers of stuff that kills on the other. The choice was not a difficult one.

So, why the small "o" in my organic gardening message? The fact is I am not a purist in this regard. I do use some synthetic (man-made) pest controls while gardening. For instance, to control weeds around mature trees or before I prepare soil for planting a new garden, I will use a product containing glysophate. This broad-spectrum weedkiller does not persist in the soil and tends not to leach out.

I also use Golfgreen fertilizer on my lawn. Yes, it contains synthetic ingredients, but it is organic-based and the nitrogen is coated with a very sophisticated slow-release ingredient. Therefore, there is very little risk of "nitrogen leachate" to contaminate the groundwater, and my lawn remains in good health.

These are my personal decisions on a subject that I take very seriously.

The organic gardening purists don't think much of my policy. But then I remind them that all things natural are not necessarily all that safe or benign. Take monkshood (*Aconitum*), foxgloves (*Digitalis*) or poisonous hemlock (*Conium maculatum*), for example. The nicotine sulphate that was removed from the market around 1970 was a completely natural extract of the tobacco plant. And there is far greater risk to local water sources if I were to spread fresh cattle or horse manure—natural products—on my lawn.

My point is that any policy based purely on black-and-white thinking is dangerous.

When you find yourself talking with someone about the controversial subject of pesticide use in the home garden, be sure to include a discussion about the use of salt on our Canadian roads in winter. Evidence suggests that we have a much greater environmental problem here than we do with home gardeners' use of pesticides. And there is an environmentally friendly alternative to road salt—calcium chloride. It just costs a little more.

What Were You Thinking?

"If gardening isn't a pleasure for you, chances are the work will merely give you a rotten disposition. If you'd rather be golfing or fishing, get a bumper sticker that says so, and forget about gardening."

—Elsa Bakalar,
A Garden of One's Own (1994)

CHAPTER 30

I have four kids and wouldn't you think that just one of them would enjoy gardening as much as I do? Not. I do have one who enjoys designing gardens. Heather is attending the University of Guelph with a major in Landscape Architecture. She loves to come home from school and walk round the garden and ask what I have been up to out there, and why I planted that there, and what is next on my list of things to build or plant. She's fond of the garden, but hasn't yet done a lot of weeding, pruning or the like. Not in our home garden, anyway.

Ben, the only boy in a family of girls, is obsessed with cars. He's always looking for a buddy at school willing to discuss his number-one love, but it is not easy to find a young teenager who is that keen to listen, and listen some more, to car talk. Truth is Ben knows more about cars than most people and God bless anyone who does know more than he does because he will pick their brain until they fall over from exhaustion. Talking about cars is the only thing that can actually take Ben's mind off his second obsession, which is food.

Last summer, our eldest, Lynn, was home from university

and enjoyed working for her mother at her yarn shop in Unionville (Mary's Yarns, slogan "Get Naturally High on Fiber!"). Knitting is Lynn's obsession—her passion for all things wool is matched only by Ben's for cars.

One day, Lynn had been watching me hoeing in the garden for a few hours. When I came in for lunch, she said, "Dad, I have been watching you out there and I am wondering, what do you think about?"

A moment went by, a very brief moment, when she answered her own question, "I know, you probably think about the same things that I think about when I'm knitting. I think about my next project."

I've noticed a funny thing about the eldest of a large family; if you wait just a moment, they will actually carry the conversation for both of you. I enjoyed my lunch and wandered back to my hoeing for a while before getting on with the next garden project that I had been rolling around in my head.

Dang! She can talk and read my mind.

My kids may not be possessed with gardening but at least they are possessed with something. All good stuff, too, I think. They say that you had better develop an interest in doing something other than work before you retire. The risk of not developing a hobby is dying early from boredom. On that score, at least a couple of my kids seem to have retirement covered. It is the in-between stage that is a mystery.

Gardening for Health

*"The garden is not an escape from reality.
It is an escape to reality."*

—Karen York,
The Holistic Garden (2001)

CHAPTER 31

Much has been said about the benefits of gardening for your health. In my 25-plus years of gardening, I've witnessed the creation of a whole new profession called horticultural therapy. This involves people—trained professionals—who bring people and gardening together in an effort to help them heal—in mind, body and/or spirit.

I picture the earth acting like a sponge for our problems. You go out, dig a hole, drop a plant in it and firm the soil around it and move on. What you leave behind is a tiny part of the stuff that was weighing heavily on you before you went out there. Well, that's how I see it anyway.

The *Globe and Mail* recently carried an interesting story about Terence Clark. He spends a lot of time in his garden. You can be sure that he is thinking of more than the birds, bees and flower fragrance while he is out there. For Clark, the production of fresh veggies in his garden has taken on new meaning; in fact, he contends it has saved his life.

You see, Terence Clark has suffered from bladder cancer for some time. Then he discovered that certain fresh fruits, vegetables and grains contain an anti-carcinogenic cocktail that can be effective in fighting certain types of cancer.

They contain antioxidant compounds that inhibit cell division and may work like a tennis doubles team matched against cancer growth: if the antioxidants don't get there first, the plant compounds may get there later.

These plant compounds could be tomorrow's cancer-fighting drugs, but until that happens, it's helpful to know that we can grow fresh vegetables in our own garden and eat them as part of a holistic approach to better health.

I'm not waiting with bated breath for the drug companies to learn how to synthesize the beneficial qualities of vegetables. It took them long enough to do this with aspirin, which originally came from the sap of the willow tree.

I will be tilling, sowing, planting and hoeing in an effort to grow my own. I'll eat what I can and give the rest away to someone needier than myself. This way I will be nourishing body and soul at one time.

Gardening as Art

"Gardening is the slowest of the performing arts."
—Mac Griswold

I have been to a few places on earth that anyone who loves to garden must absolutely visit in his or her lifetime. One is the bulb-growing fields of the Netherlands. Timing, of course, is critical. A summer trip may be comfortable, with the lovely cool North Sea breeze and all. But to really get the show, you must go during the last couple of weeks of April or the first week of May. This is your window of opportunity for the show of a lifetime and your chance to outwit Mother Nature. If it is an early spring, you will catch the late tulips during the first week of May and if it is a late spring, you will see the crocuses and hyacinths during the third week of April. Everything else just falls into place. Never mind the cold and the rain (which will happen, for sure). Dress for it.

Your flight into Amsterdam's Schiphol Airport on a clear day will provide you with your first postcard snapshot of what's in store. I have been four times in my life and plan to return.

Another place wild horses should not keep you from is the second largest annual flower show in the world at Hampton Court, about an hour northwest of London, England. It occurs during the first full week of July and is a very different experience from Holland and for that matter, any other garden event (even the crowded Chelsea Flower Show in London, which I have attended twice).

It is huge—about 3.2 hectares (eight acres). It is colourful.

The Brits know their plants and how to show them off. Even a plate of tomatoes is a work of art. It is so intense you will need to take lots of pictures; a notebook is also recommended. There is abundant information and such broad horticultural expertise you'll find a society for every imaginable genus of garden plant, including the Toad Lily Society (it's hard to say that and keep a straight face, but there must be some serious toad lily fanciers out there). Take at least two full days to get around—the first to scout the place and the second to return to your favourite areas to drink in more knowledge and eye candy.

The other place that you absolutely would be denying yourself to miss is Monet's Gardens at Giverny in France. I have never been as inspired by one garden as I was by his. It has been beautifully restored with an eye to the way it was when he died in 1926, and is maintained to perfection.

I loved the rose arbour and the lily pond—looking just as he painted them. And the espaliered apple fence inspired me to go home and plant one just like it, only about 90 years younger. You will also see some very interesting uses of ornamental grasses (and you thought they were a new idea!), ground covers and the creation of "rooms." Go any time that suits you from late March through fall as I believe this garden will look good for eight months of the year.

The experience of visiting Giverny is multi-dimensional: Monet's home is an inspiration, and his artwork speaks for itself. It is this unique combination of experiences that will draw me back. This, and the fact that the man who made such a powerful mark in the annals of art history actually considered himself a gardener first, an artist second.

To Lawn or Not to Lawn

*"Consider the many special delights a lawn affords:
soft mattress for a creeping baby; worm hatchery for a
robin; croquet or badminton court; baseball diamond;
restful green perspectives leading the eye to a background
of flower border, shrubs, or hedge; green shadows—'This
lawn, a carpet all alive/ With shadows flung from leaves' —
as changing and spellbinding as the waves of the seas."*

—Katherine S. White,
Onward and Upward in the Garden (1979)

CHAPTER 33

I ask you, what stirs more controversy these days than the topic of lawns? My dad would say that it's wise never to discuss two topics: children and religion. Better to keep your opinions to yourself rather than risk a friendship. I suggest doing the same where lawns are concerned.

Except for me. I don't like to turn my back on a reasonable risk, if the result is some constructive thought and discussion on a subject that's close to my heart.

Just about everywhere I go, I run into what I call the "conspiracy against the lawn." There is a wellspring of discontent with our favourite living green carpet and all activity associated with the maintenance and growth of it. Much of the criticism is legitimate. Lawn mowers and weed-whackers, for instance, produce more airborne toxins than cars do.

However, before I give the critics too much credit, it is my opinion that of all the ground covers in the world, there is none more sophisticated than the lawn. Look around and you will notice that public parks and the space around many commercial buildings are carpeted in grass. If there were a more effective alternative, a living plant that took the rigours of foot traffic, wouldn't they have used that?

Which brings up the subject of golf. My son Ben works summers at the local golf course. His supervisor (we'll call him Larry) doesn't think much of my regular messages on my Saturday morning radio show in Toronto. He feels that I have been endorsing the concept of growing a lawn without the use of chemical pesticides just a little too much.

Perhaps he is a bit battle-scarred. Golf course maintenance people have long been criticized for using an excess of chemical pesticides and fertilizers. They also get their knuckles rapped for their generous use of water for irrigation.

Larry felt so strongly that he wrote me a letter to give his side of the story. Here is a summary of his points:

·"The word 'pesticide' has developed a bad name: what the word really means is that the product has been tested, proven to be safe and proven to do what the label says it will do. I might add that our federal government does have a record of being more stringent in its regulations and control of registered pesticides than any other country in the western world.

· "Since 'organic' lawn-care products have become popular, 'snake oil' salespeople have increased exponentially. Their products generally lack university testing, just word-of-mouth endorsements from so and so down the road."

Larry tells of a guy who sells a product made up entirely of fish parts. While this sounds environmentally friendly and safe, Larry points out that mercury from the environment builds up in fish. The older the fish, the more mercury they contain. The fish by-product in fertilizer has not, according to Larry, been tested, so how safe is it really? Mercury is an effective fungicide but was banned in Canada more than 10 years ago.

Larry adds that his golf greens, at the demand of golfers, are cut at 2.3 mm (less than 1/8th of an inch)! He says, "The poor grass plant doesn't have a chance against attack of fungus. In a home lawn cut at the recommended 7.6 cm (three inches), fungal diseases, while present, are barely noticeable and seldom if ever require treatment."

Golf course superintendents and greenskeepers are between a rock and a hard place, trying to produce a near-perfect lawn for golfers while minimizing the use of chemicals and maintenance techniques that harm the environment. Unless people are going to simply give up the sport, which is not going to happen any time soon, I think that it is better to encourage the Larrys of the world to act as responsibly as they possibly can, and to continue to look for more environmentally friendly ways of doing what they need to do.

Some people think that we should allow all our lawns to go natural—that we just mind our own business and let Mother Nature do what she will with the real estate. Well, it's not that easy, because more than 60 percent of the plants that naturalize in open soil are noxious weeds, introduced by none other than the human race.

I favour a far less radical approach to the proper management of green spaces: let's continue to pull back on the use of pesticides while we explore other plant species that can do the job and let's encourage cultural practices for lawn maintenance that meet our standards for a greener, healthier world.

Truth is, great strides have been made in recent years in this direction so let's keep it up! The goal is in sight.

The alternative I fear the most if we don't is more asphalt. Ouch!

Know Your Friends

"He leapt the fence and saw that all nature was a garden."

–Horace Walpole, on landscape designer William Kent,
On Modern Gardening (1780)

CHAPTER 34

This past weekend, a python was found in Toronto on a very busy street corner. Someone called 911 and the police arrived. They didn't like what they saw and decided to call in Animal Control.

When the brave souls who catch wild and stray animals for a living arrived, they took one look at the beast, which was over two metres (6 1/2 feet) long, and said, 'This isn't our department." And left it alone.

Meanwhile, another cop had arrived. He immediately exclaimed, "Hey, if nobody wants this pet snake, I'll take it!" There was no objection when he bent over, picked up the snake and put it in the trunk of his vehicle, next to his emergency kit and the teddy bears for giving to stressed-out kids.

This morning, there is a picture in the newspaper of this hero-cop with the python wrapped around his head—and a big smile on his face. You can only imagine what the snake was thinking.

Now here is a guy who knows who his friends are, or at least he knows whom he can trust.

Gardeners should be so sensitive. Many otherwise intelligent people are scared silly at the sight of some of the most helpful garden critters, including native snakes (the venomous kinds notwithstanding). Did you know that a common garter snake consumes a whole lot of garden slugs, moles, mice and small rats?

Many other garden critters are equally useful allies in the battle to maintain a beautiful garden. Take spiders and big black beetles, for example, which eat all kinds of pesky bugs. And where did we ever get the idea that toads give us warts? Some old wives' tales never die. The garden toad is a voracious eater—slugs go down so nice when you are a toad—and flying insects like mosquitoes, house flies and aphids are also high on the menu.

Frogs fall in the same category as toads, yet most people have a real fear of picking up a frog. If you are patient and watch a frog long enough, you will actually see it flick out its tongue and catch a fly or mosquito in mid-air. How amazing is that?

Bats also suffer from a lot of bad press. Something about rabies and sucking blood. Actually, bats are less responsible for the spread of rabies than domestic dogs, which pick the disease up from other dogs, often wild ones. And there are no documented cases of bats sucking human blood, at least not in Canada.

During one warm summer evening of feeding, a bat will consume its full body weight in mosquitoes and other flying insects. That sounds pretty good to me. When I learned this, I nailed up a couple of bat houses in a tall backyard tree; the bat house should be at least six metres (20 feet) off the ground to attract residents. It obviously worked because I have seen bats doing their fly-by after the sun goes down on many occasions.

By the way, bats do not get tangled in your hair either; their sonar is too sophisticated for that! Nonetheless, they are feared by many people.

But there you go. There isn't always a lot of logic or reason behind what we do or what we believe.

As adults, isn't it our job to separate the good guys from the garden pests? Dispelling myths about helpful but maligned critters is another mission that gardeners need to take on. It definitely pays to know who your friends are.

As for a python in the yard, I am not so sure.

Compost Poster Boy

> *"One thing that unites all gardeners as they contemplate the compost heap is a belief in reincarnation, at least for plants."*
>
> **—Geoffrey Charlesworth,**
> *The Opinionated Gardener* (1988)

For a few years I worked with my friend Dan Matheson on CTV's popular news/magazine show, *Canada AM*, doing a weekly gardening segment. We got to know each other quite well, especially as we touched on some pretty personal stuff over our time on the air. Like compost.

Now compost may not be very personal to you, but it is near and dear to my heart. As Dan came to know this, he began calling me the "compost poster boy," a moniker that I was actually quite proud of. It may come as a surprise that there are many people around who are passionate about compost. We just aren't very good at advertising.

The passion, I believe, takes time to develop. First you have to try it. Get a compost bin and fill it with raw organic material, brown leaves and chopped branch trimmings layered with smaller quantities of green stuff like grass clippings and kitchen scraps (avoid animal fat and meat). Water it from time to time and wait.

What will transpire in a few months is a wonderful metamorphosis of nature-our banana peels will break down to become rich, friable compost of the highest order, a natural fertilizer that will assist any plant reach its greatest potential.

CHAPTER 35

Simply spread the finished compost around the roots of a perennial, shrub or tree or in your vegetable garden.

This exercise should not be mistaken for feeding plants; in fact, you are feeding the soil, enriching it so the plant can draw on the nutrients and minerals in the soil to feed itself through photosynthesis (another miracle!).

The beauty of the process is that you have little to do other than pile up the raw materials and perform minor maintenance. Mother Nature provides all the grunt work through gangs of active microbes. While this is an immensely complicated process from a scientific point of view, you don't have to have to be a scientist to enjoy the benefits.

(A friend of mine says his son is one of those people who, if you ask him the time, will tell you how to build a watch. For those who want to delve deeper into composting, check out the book I wrote with Lorraine Johnson called *The Real Dirt*. Highly recommended bedtime reading if you want a really good night's sleep!).

I happen to think that compost is the answer to so many of the world's problems.

Take municipal waste, for example. The city of Edmonton has been composting on a massive scale for a few years; in fact, it boasts the largest composting facility in the world (I've toured it and it really is incredible). Using different technologies from around the world to build a monster "digester," they have eliminated the need for landfills. You read right—they no longer bury their garbage! (Digging a big hole to put all our trash into is crazy; the costs continue for generations after the garbage is covered up.)

The finished product is considered grade-B compost, which means that they use it to cover up old landfills, complete highway embankments, etc. Brilliant-expensive to build in the first place, but brilliant.

The Edmonton experience inspired the good folks in Hamilton, Ont., to build a similar, smaller composting facility. I'm hoping this is a trend. My friend Susan Antler, Executive Director of the Composting Council of Canada, claims that it is. She says that some smartly run municipalities are beginning to think of their waste as a resource, not waste at all. And that, to me, is the best part—a complete change of mind and attitude about the stuff that is left over after we have enjoyed ourselves.

Since my days with Dan Matheson, I have been working with *Canada AM*'s funny man Jeff Hutchison. Though he doesn't refer to me as "compost poster boy," he gets great pleasure from introducing me with, "And now a new episode of CSI—Compost Scene Investigation!"

I'm sure that someone finds this amusing.

Space of Your Own

"A garden is the interface
between the house and the rest of civilization."

—Geoffrey Charlesworth,
A Gardener Obsessed (1994)

CHAPTER 36

My fondest memories of the family home were of the tree fort that my dad built in the large apple tree in the backyard. You see, that was my space. I could go up there and be king of the yard. Not only that, I got a grand view of the garden, too. Maybe all I did was dream and make-believe but, for a kid, that is quite a luxury.

When I grew older and had kids of my own, I still valued my own space.

At the side of our house, right next to my four compost bins, I built a wonderful escape that everyone thought was just a garden shed. You could easily make that mistake as it was filled with garden tools, bags of potting soil and stuff like that. I didn't tell anyone in the family this, but I purposely designed my escape so I could stretch a rope hammock from one corner to the other.

There is nothing—and I mean nothing—that I enjoy more on a warm summer afternoon than to lie in there and listen to the rain fall on the roof. No phone calls, no e-mails and no kids. Just me, the sounds of the rain and the birds and the temptation of a cold beer within arm's reach.

Dr. John Gray, who wrote the bestselling book, *Men Are*

From Mars, Women Are From Venus, would call this my cave. The idea is that I, being a man, value a place where I can go and contemplate the state of my universe. And not talk or have to listen, except of course to the birds, etc.

All this may sound very selfish, especially the part about being away from the kids. But call it what you want, we all need a little space at some time. And kids do, too. I think my dad understood that when he built the tree fort for me in the backyard.

If you have kids, I suggest you create some space in the yard for them to dream and play make-believe. For my son Ben, it was the sandbox (see Chapter 5). For my daughters, it was the enclosed play gym. However small your yard, it can provide the potential to launch a rocket to the moon. Or Mars.

And when your kids grow up, they can think back and say, "Yes, I too was king of the yard!"

Just the Facts

*"Men are like plants which never flourish
if they are not well cultivated."*

—Charles Louis de Secondat, Baron de Montesquieu,
The Persian Letters (1721)

CHAPTER 37

We have known that gardens and people have enjoyed a symbiotic relationship for generations. We create a garden in partnership with Mother Nature; we benefit from the experience of doing it, and living with it, for as long as we enjoy our time together.

All that mushy stuff about feeling good every time we go out into the garden is obvious to those of us who love it; the hard sell is convincing the rest of the world that these benefits are for all.

But there is a growing weight of scientific evidence to support what we all know in our gardening hearts. Most recently, Oladele ("Dele") Ogunseitan, a social ecologist at the University of California, Irvine, has paired science and psychology to give us tangible research results about how plants, flowers and green landscapes affect both physical and mental health. He developed a groundbreaking method for measuring the relationship between a person's environment and their mental well-being. It was difficult, says Ogunseitan, because "most people cannot easily express why they have preferences for these locations. The problem is that we tend to co-mingle sensory information, meaning that we register colours, smells and other senses all together."[*]

The results are fascinating.

For instance, in one of his studies, "flowers and large bodies of water were the most common mental-health enhancing features."* This has implications for health care, and reinforces the work done by Roger Ulrich, architecture professor at Texas A&M—if we design hospitals with lots of windows looking out on water and colourful flowers, patients will feel better and get out faster.

Other studies by researchers such as Rachel and Stephen Kaplan have delved into the restorative effect of nature and found that just being in a green space for a short while helps to improve concentration. Now you know why every downtown parkette is packed with office workers at lunchtime!

On another front, Dr. B.C. Wolverton, a NASA scientist, who has done much research connecting plants with better air quality, has recommended "that two plants per 10 square metres (107 square feet) can greatly improve interior environments."*

Studies by the Human-Environmental Resources Laboratory found that "inner-city crime rates were lower in apartments with green surroundings; those with high amounts of greenery had 48 percent fewer property crimes and 56 percent fewer violent crimes. Inner-city families with trees and greenery in their immediate surroundings had safer domestic environments."*

These are the facts, folks.

If you have a passion for gardening, chances are that you knew all this intuitively and I'm preaching to the converted.

But knowing the facts may give you the confirmation that you were looking for; now you can spread the word.

The challenge is to get this information into the hands of the doubtful ones. They need to have it lodged into their hard drives. Health care professionals need to see it. Politicians and government bureaucrats need to see it.

We need to treat this information like the crown jewels of horticultural facts and help the rest of the world grow better in every sense.

*www.growertalks.com, archive article #1384.

I Take the Veggie Car!

"A true gardener must be brutal—
and imaginative for the future."

corn-derived fibre socks to Japan to compete with low-cost textile manufacturers in China and other Asian nations.**

No word on how many times you can wash the corn socks or how long you can wear them before they disintegrate, but I'm sure someone thought about that before they loaded them into the container.

As state of the art as all this is, credit must be given to the founder of the Ford Motor Company, Henry Ford. In the 1930s, he experimented with using soybeans in car parts, in particular as a replacement for sheet metal. Born into a farming family, Ford was determined to marry his unprecedented success in the car business with his passion for agriculture. Unfortunately, very little ever came of it.

So many of the clothes that we wear—from cotton chinos to silk pyjamas—and things we use everyday—wicker chairs, sisal mats, corks, this book—have roots in the plant business. There's no telling how far the turnip car and corn socks will take us.

Computer screens from plant resins, asphalt from hemp, rubber tires from the sap of a tree-oh yeah, we did that, didn't we?

I can't wait to see what's next.

* "The Veggie Car?" ,*The Globe and Mail*, December 17, 2005

** *The National Post*, November 9, 2005.

Biomimicry
and What It Means to You

"Those who labour in the earth are the chosen people of God, if ever he had a chosen people."

—Thomas Jefferson,
Notes on the State of Virginia (1782)

CHAPTER 39

Here is a trend that is having a big impact on the gardening world: biomimicry. Simply put, biomimicry is innovation inspired by nature. This is not about making silk flowers.

The classic example is Velcro. Remember the story of how it was "discovered"? In the 1940s, Swiss mountaineer George de Mestral was pulling burrs off his pants when he looked closely at their clever little hooks and thought, "Hey! This concept could be useful!"

Now comes the UltraCane⁵ which was inspired by bats. This walking cane for the visually impaired uses ultrasonic signals which bounce off objects in the environment and feed information back to the cane. Covering the area in front up to head height, the cane alerts the user to obstacles, making walking down the street much less risky.*

Where gardening is concerned, we should always be considering what nature can teach us. It is an opportunity to become a part of, rather than apart from, the genius available to us through the natural world.

William McDonough, a world renowned eco-architect, says there is plenty of free energy around without the use of oil or nuclear-generated power; this energy arrives here each day in the form of sunlight. In fact, the solar energy the earth receives equals more than 5,000 times the energy that we use from all other sources combined. What we have to do is learn how to harness this energy effectively.

Speaking of "sun power," here is a thought-provoking opinion on the subject:

According to Janine Benyus, a British biologist and life sciences writer, we can learn profound lessons from the process of photosynthesis. "A leaf has tens of thousand of photosynthetic reaction centres," she says. "They're like molecular scale solar batteries operating at 93 percent quantum efficiency, which means that for every hundred particles of light (solar energy) that strikes the leaf, 93 are turned into sugars. That's stellar in terms of effectiveness. Better still, these solar cells are manufactured silently, in water, and without toxins."***

Leaves, no different from the ones in your yard, are being looked at by scientists and engineers to help design smaller, more efficient power cells.

What we can learn from nature is not limited to solar energy, of course. We can look at virtually every aspect of our gardening experience through the prism of our natural world for direction and answers. A deeper understanding of nature's workings can only make us better gardeners.

As Benyus says, "One of the many gifts of biomimicry is that you enter into deep conversations with organisms, and this student-elder dialogue absolutely fills you with awe. Seeing nature as model, measure and mentor changes the very way you view and value the natural world. Instead of seeing nature as warehouse, you begin to see her as teacher. Instead of valuing what you can extract from her, you value what you can learn from her."

Wow. I couldn't have said it better myself.

*Gardens Illustrated, April, 2006.

**www.biomimicry.org

And the Seasons, They Go Round and Round

"We don't take time to experience the experience."

–Barbara Moses,
The Globe and Mail

It is late fall as I write this and my garden has just about been put to bed. In fact, I can't think of anything else that I need to do right now, but after that first big snowfall, I'm sure I'll come up with all kinds of things I've forgotten.

As the season is winding down, the neighbourhood horticultural society held its annual fall perennial swap. Kim Hooper was one of those who showed up early at the sale and left with a bundle of assorted plants, including a few rare varieties. "I love gardening, it's my passion," she told a reporter from the local community newspaper. "It's peaceful, therapeutic and it teaches patience."

Kim seems to understand all that is so fundamental to great gardening experiences, but for the next four or five months, she will have to be content with gardening in her head.

The rhythm of winter changes us. While the orbit of earth actually brings us closer to the sun, its tilting axis means that days are shorter. My evenings in the garden become a memory. I think I'm sleeping more, and certainly have less energy after dinner. Sitting and reading for two or three hours seems like a perfectly respectable use of time, where three months ago I wouldn't even have considered it.

Many birds are migrating south. Cardinals, which

generally like their independence, stay home and are now flocking together. I find it curious that woodpeckers begin courting shortly after Christmas. How do they court in -15°C temperatures, I wonder?

This time of year, I like to dig out gardening books that I haven't looked at for a long time. Seed catalogues begin arriving and I read and re-read them before making considered choices about the seeds and summer bulbs that I will order too many of. Come March, when the first of several serious thaws occur, I will begin to get restless. This is my personal celebration of the season ahead—restless sleep and a yearning to get to work. The planting season will be much too busy to even think about what I think about through the winter months.

As of today, Mary and I are planning our Christmas celebrations with family, friends and business associates. This is one of those very few periods in our annual calendar that we can take the time to catch up with them, to have discussions that we don't have at any other time of year. Those who are normally a little outside our day-to-day life seem closer at the end of the holiday season.

And I ask myself, why does it seem appropriate—that we do all of this visiting, reading and contemplation this time of year? It's because we have the time. Because, really, there is nothing to do in the garden, so what is the alternative?

Through the winter, I'm very grateful for this country, my growing zone (5) and the distinct changing of seasons that occurs here. I wouldn't have it any other way.

No Such Thing
as Failure in the Garden

"Never, never, never, never give up."

—Winston Churchill,
1950

There's nothing that I enjoy about my work as much as meeting the public. Writing, broadcasting and developing new gardening products take a lot of my time but when I can get out of the office and my own garden to listen to stories and engage with Canadian gardeners face to face, I always enjoy it to bits.

I have been doing this for over 25 years and have learned a lot about our gardening priorities and concerns. For one, we are a modest bunch. Many times people have prefaced a gardening question with an apology like, "I can't grow a thing" or "I have a black thumb." Given a chance I like to reply, "I am here to fix that!"

My very existence as a garden communicator hinges on connecting with people at a level that helps them to understand that gardening knows no boundaries or borders. Anyone can do it and everyone who does can benefit from it. All that stands in our way is an attitude that discourages attempts at getting our knees dirty and growing things.

This handicap is the result of avoiding failure at almost any cost. Take work, for example. How many times in a business day do we celebrate our falling short of our original goal or missing a deadline or disappointing the boss? Never. And yet, I have met a lot of successful people who say they have learned a lot more from their failures than from their successes.

Have you noticed how many times a baby will fall while attempting to get to its feet?   How often does a one- or two-year-old reach out to touch-everything! A dog, a cat, the toaster—and they learn something every time.

At some point in our development as adults we learn to pull back, to take our time before jumping into something. We basically unlearn to take risks. Which is where the garden comes in. Here is a place where you can make mistakes and they really don't count for much, not in a negative sense anyway.

I planted the shady area in the backyard of our previous house several times. The shade under the canopy of mature trees was a real problem for me. It turns out the real challenge was not the shade but the competition of the tree roots. It took me 11 years to figure out a combination of plants that worked back there and looked good. I can't tell you how many plants I killed in the meantime. Lesson learned.

If you have difficulty taking a risk, take a few in your garden. In fact, take lots of risks! No one will judge you for your failures and you will learn much more than the person who never pushed the boundaries. And if something dies, remember my first rule of the garden: "There are no failures here, just composting opportunities."

Home Remedies

"Only you can do it. But you don't have to do it alone."
—Brian Dalzell

It seems that we are forever looking for alternatives to the problem-solvers sold on the garden-centre shelves. Perhaps we just don't trust whatever it is they put in the package. The bottle or box contains-well, usually something you can't pronounce and if you can, you have no idea of what it means or does.

Where pesticides are concerned, a whole different language exists. It is meant to be technical and specialized because that is the precise nature of the pest-control business. Perhaps this is why people look for alternatives that they understand and trust not to be harmful to kids, pets or the environment. And why one of the best-liked features of my weekly radio show is the recipes for home remedies I frequently give out. Maybe listeners enjoy preparing these concoctions in the kitchen while listening to the radio.

My most popular home-grown recipe is for this general-purpose insect spray that is very effective against aphids and other common indoor plant pests:

　　1 garlic bulb
　　1 small onion
　　15 ml (1 tbsp) cayenne pepper
　　1 liter (4 cups) water
　　15 ml (1 tbsp) liquid soap detergent

Chop and grind the garlic and onion, add the cayenne pepper and mix with the water. Let the mixture steep one hour, then add the liquid soap detergent (it helps the formula stick to the leaves of the plants). Filter the liquid through a cloth and apply with an atomizer or sprayer when needed. Store in a tightly covered jar in the refrigerator up to one week.

To discourage moles:

50 ml (1/5 cup) castor oil
30 ml (2 tbsp) liquid dishwashing detergent
90 ml (6 tbsp) water.

Whip together castor oil and detergent in a blender until the mixture is the consistency of shaving cream. Add water and whip together again. Take a regular garden watering can, fill it with warm water, add 30 ml (2 tbsp) of the oil mixture and stir. Sprinkle immediately over the areas of greatest mole infestation. For best results, apply after a rain or thorough watering.

It can be fun to make homemade remedies from kitchen ingredients but be aware that lots of things we use domestically are not appropriate for use in the garden. Just because something is natural doesn't mean it's benign. Nicotine, for example, is extremely poisonous, and anything with bleach in it makes me nervous.

The best advice that I can give is this: if you feel the need to use a pesticide in your garden, be sure to read the label and understand what the product is intended to do. Keep kids and pets away, even if you use homemade remedies.

And consider another easy alternative—doing nothing. There is a natural rhythm to all things in the garden and if you wait a while, chances are pretty good that the pest will move on, die a natural death or be eaten by something else.

Remember that over 95 percent of the bugs in your garden are deemed "good" bugs (pesticides don't differentiate, killing good with the bad). Add to this the many helpful predators out there, such as toads, frogs, moles (yes, moles), snakes and birds, and you realize that there are a lot of good guys on our side.

Not bad odds if you ask me.

I Love to Dig!

"The best place to seek God is in the garden. You can dig for him there."

—George Bernard Shaw,
The Adventures of The Black Girl and Her Search For God. (1932)

I had the privilege of growing up with gardening. My dad, Len, had a passion for it that almost defied description. He was, after all, the only person I know of who kissed evergreens—all the time! Without apology.

One day in 1986, when I was barely 30, I took a walk with Dad through the valley of his public show garden, Cullen Gardens and Miniature Village in Whitby, Ont. It was one of those lovely early fall days when the temperature is perfect to be outdoors. There were no bugs to speak of, which was really something in that mosquito-infested cedar forest. We just walked and talked. Him, walking with his favourite D-handled spade, and me, just trying to keep up the pace of both the conversation and the walk.

On most such occasions, our conversations revolved almost exclusively around business. Even the topic of gardening was always discussed in the context of the family business. So it came as a great surprise to me on this particular day when he stopped abruptly during our stroll, mid-stride. He bent down, took a stance that I had seen thousands of times before, and he began to dig. Right in the middle of the dirt path. One spadeful. A second. A third. Then he moved the dirt back into the new hole with the spade.

CHAPTER 43

He slowly straightened his back, hand on the bottom of his spine for support. Slightly out of breath, he said, "I love to dig." Then he paused. "I love to dig," he said again. Then he looked me square in the eye and exclaimed in case I hadn't heard him, "I LOVE to dig, Mark!"

Wow, I thought. My dad really is kind of nuts. Expressing such passion over a basic thing like digging was unusual even for him. There was no doubt in my mind that he was good at it. There is a particular skill to digging. The position of your feet, the spacing of your arms on the shaft of the spade, the thrust of the blade into the ground, pushing your shoulders into it-all factor into a satisfying digging experience. Not to mention that the spade itself must be clean, and sharp as a butcher knife, and it helps if it is worn with use—the oils from your hands having smoothed the wooden shaft to a working finish. This is a tool without a price, because you can't buy one. You create it through practice.

After our memorable digging experience, about 10 or 12 years went by. It took this long for me to begin to understand what he was talking about that autumn day in the valley. Over that time, I had planned and planted my own garden—a few times. I had learned to take the time to slow down and dig my own soil. To smell it in the moist spring, the hot, dry summer and the coolness of autumn.

I had spent many autumn days turning finished compost into my garden soil. I rescued more than a few earthworms from the blade of my spade. And I would rest on the D handle of it after a good dig. Time and practice caused the experience of digging to slowly sink into my being...until one day I got it.

There is a great joy to digging soil.

Today, there is an English spade hanging in my toolshed that I treasure above all of my garden tools. It has a fine metal blade that holds an edge when sharpened; made of Sheffield steel, it bends rather than breaks when pressured. It slices through soil like a hot knife through butter. It is such a favourite of mine that it has appeared in more of my TV shows than my kids have. And they don't make them any more (the spade, of course, not the kids).

One of the most difficult decisions I will have to make someday is which of our four kids I will leave this spade to. The spade given to me by my dad the day I left home. Perhaps one day, while walking and talking about ordinary things with one of our precious children, or perhaps while digging, it will come to me. Just as my dad opened my eyes to something that I had always considered ordinary, the soil will speak to me.

And I will know just what to do.

But Why Do You Do It?

*"No two gardens are the same.
No two days are the same in one garden."*
—Hugh Johnson

The U.S. National Garden Bureau in Illinois, has come up with the top 10 reasons why people love to garden. The subject fascinates me because I love to garden myself and often wonder where this powerful pull of the garden comes from.

Here are the reasons that gardening is the number-one leisure time activity, according to the NGB:*

1. Garden for safe, healthy food.
A lot of us worry about what is in the canned, frozen and even the fresh food that we eat from the grocery store. Growing your own provides the opportunity to control the process and ensures that the food you put in your mouth contains only what you want it to contain.

2. Garden for exercise.
According to the NGB, studies show that "an hour of moderate gardening can burn up to 300 calories for women and almost 400 for men." Pushing a lawn mower is good. Pushing a manual push mower is even better! Bending and stooping in the garden provide all of the benefits of a good stretch without getting bored (I can relate to this as I hate to take the time to stretch even though I know it's good for you.)

3. Garden to add beauty.

This one seems so obvious I am surprised it's not at the top of the list. Indoors, plants enhance a room, improve the air—making it easier to breathe—and tempt one to linger longer. Outdoors, plants provide colour, texture, shade, motion, a home for birds and other wildlife, and the list grows on!

4. Garden to learn.

The more you know, the more you want to know. In my case, the more I learn, the more I realize how little I know. Which makes me want to learn some more. For me, gardening is like eating salted peanuts; the more I have, the more I want. And at the end of it all a cold beer never tasted so good (don't ask what I learn from that.).

5. Garden to make money.

I have seen this so many times. Someone enjoys gardening as a hobby and before you know it they are working at a local garden centre. Or they start to grow plants for "profit" (which is as misleading a statement as I can make). Anyone who goes looking for employment as a result of a positive gardening experience is doing so for the very best reason of all—they love it. As a Chinese proverb says: "If you love your work, you won't work a day in your life."

6. Garden to meet people.

Sharing your gardening experience and knowledge with others is a great way to widen your social circle. I like to say that gardening is the best cure for shyness. I have frequently seen a person who is otherwise a "wallflower" become engaged in conversation about gardening, and they appear so relaxed and natural. Which is the secret to great conversation. Next time you have a party, invite some gardeners just to ensure that there will be lots of lively conversation.

7. Garden to be creative.
I like to say that designing a garden is not only a creative endeavour but also perhaps the only art form that you will never finish. Have you ever met a gardener who, rubbing their hands together, exclaimed, "There, I'm done with that!" then moved on to learning the next thing—sailing, golfing or whatever? It just doesn't work like that. The fact is anyone who thinks they have mastered gardening is not a master gardener.

8. Garden to win.
If you have a competitive streak, gardening may appeal to you as a friendly way to show off your gardening skills. Growers of the largest pumpkin, the sweetest tomato or the most outrageous dahlia seem to be attracted to our hobby for the personal satisfaction of beating others at the game. This is a reason for gardening that I have some trouble relating to: I have never entered any of my produce or plants in a competition. My daughter Emma put her white pumpkin in the Markham Fair once, though, and won 4th prize. I will admit to feeling a twinge of pride at the time. Perhaps gardening to win also applies to "beating Mother Nature"—trying against all odds to grow a plant that may not be considered hardy in our zone, for example. Damn the torpedoes anyway!

9. Garden for emotional needs and spiritual connections.
So often in our lives, our garden is a sanctuary. This is where you go to think, to dream, to weep and to wallow in the joy of a unique outdoor experience. I believe the garden can help to mend broken hearts and to inspire us to great things.

10. Garden for lasting memories.
Children can enjoy being in the garden and being involved in the garden. Whether you have a pot or two of flowering plants or a large garden, the memories created there in the formative minds of young people should not be underestimated. Many of the conversations I have had with people over the years have begun with some reference to gardens and plants they remember from their childhood.

There are probably as many reasons to garden as there are gardeners but I'd say many of us can identify with this list. Most of the time it is good enough for me to know that there is no place I would rather be. Now where's my hoe?
I have work to do.

A Fragile Steeplechase

"Work as if you live in the early days of a better nation."
—Alasdair Gray

I live on a farm and enjoy gardening on a four-hectare (10-acre) parcel of land that offers almost unlimited access to topsoil. You might think I could mine this stuff forever and always enjoy a fabulous garden. Alas, anything but.

Every spring, I spread compost from my rather sizeable collection of composters over the surface of the soil in my perennial beds. My veggie garden gets the green-manure treatment every second year—I plant either buckwheat or clover, let it grow up and then till it in to enrich the soil. This principle of feeding the soil is crucial. If you want a living organism to grow, flourish and remain healthy, you have to feed it, right? Well, while the soil (with help from the sun and water) does feed your plants, it is also a living organism in itself. It isn't just a layer of inert "dirt" that happens to cover a good portion of the planet.

In fact, it takes a hundred years to create 2.5 cm (one inch) of soil, so it's not something to take for granted or to squander. I believe that gardeners who understand this are among the very best advocates for saving and enriching the precious little soil we have remaining on earth.

In a 1999 issue of *Eco-Farm & Garden* magazine, botanist and agricultural expert Diana Beresford-Kroeger writes, "Soil is more, much more (than merely a place to grow plants). It is the underground city of microscopic banking and swapping of chemicals essential to all life. It is the fragile steeplechase upon which all animal survival depends. It is trees on their knees, begging the fungi in a microrrhizal prayer for growth. It is the domination of the soil kingdom by allelochemicals. It is war and it is peace and it is prey."*

Wow. You could use that quote to open the next meeting of your local horticultural society and leave everyone very impressed (even if they don't understand all the terms she uses). Beresford-Kroeger goes on to say, "Building good soil is the organic grower's task. It is the true prerequisite to all successful gardening and farming, for without a good, healthy soil, growing is next to impossible."*

All organic gardeners agree that feeding our soil is our number-one responsibility. Healthy soil should pass what I call the "chocolate cake test." Get out there and dig some holes in your soil for the fun of it. If it isn't fun, i.e., if you can't slice through the soil like rich, dark chocolate cake, then you need to get busy and start feeding it lots of organic matter and, if you have clay soil, some sharp sand as well.

Another indicator of healthy soil is the presence of lots of earthworms. They enrich the soil with their castings, and aerate it as they tunnel through it, allowing water and air to reach plant roots. If you add a layer of organic matter (like shredded leaves) to the soil surface, the worms will do all the work for you.

Beresford-Kroeger calls healthy soil the "elemental bedrock—an oxygen-rich matrix" of the garden. Hang on her words, oh faithful organic gardeners!

Eloquent language aside, I will continue to spread compost on my flower beds and sow clover and buckwheat in the veggie garden, knowing that I am minimizing the need to control pests and diseases. Healthy soil equals healthy plants with much greater resistance to both.

If you forget everything you have heard about creating a beautiful garden but this one bit of advice about feeding the soil, you have a future here.

Photo: Emma Cullen

I'm Goin' to Britain in My Mind

"Gardens are Britain's
greatest contribution to the visual arts."
—Nikolaus Pevsner (1944)

James Taylor, one of my favourite musicians, sings a song with the line "I'm goin' to Carolina in my mind." I frequently find myself whistling it while in the garden. The tune is catchy but the trouble I have with the lyrics is that I have never been to Carolina, so going there in my mind is a bit tricky. But I have been to Britain and my mind drifts over there with no problem at all.

Although this book is subtitled "Personal Reflections on the Canadian Gardening Experience," it would not be complete without a reflection on British gardens. The immeasurable passion the Brits have for gardening draws me there at least once a year.

Last year, I travelled there with my family in March and found the time to visit Kew Gardens in southwest London. Despite the fact that none of my kids have an interest in gardening, they seemed to enjoy a stroll around the masses of crocuses that coloured the great expanse of lawns.

Four months later, I was back in London, this time with my good friend Denis Flanagan, to attend one of the greatest annual British garden showcases, the Hampton Court Palace Flower Show. For one solid and very hot day, we walked the show, trying not to miss anything. We took notes and hundreds of photographs, then returned for a second full day to go at a slower pace and really study the exhibits that tickled our fancy. "This is Britain," I said to myself. A country of gardens.

I recall seeing some statistics produced by the Netherlands Bulb Information Centre in the late 1980s charting how many spring-flowering bulbs were planted per capita by nation. Curiously, Canada ranked in the mid-range at about three times that of the United States. At the top of the list was, you guessed it, Great Britain. At the time the Brits planted almost five times as many bulbs per person as Canadians did, and 15 times more than the Americans. They even beat the Dutch at their own game, proving that the award for bulb-mania belonged to the British. Evidence suggests that little has changed; if anything, they are more obsessed with gardening than ever.

I'm a member of Britain's Royal Horticultural Society (RHS) and receive its monthly magazine called *The Garden* (who but the British would claim authority over a title like that!). It is a wonderful publication that I read from cover to cover before passing it on to my mother-in-law.

In a recent issue of *The Garden*, there was an announce-ment that the RHS has sanctioned a new organization called ThinkinGardens. Its purpose is to advance the discussion of the role of gardens in British society through publications, events and discussions.

In the manifesto of ThinkinGardens, the founders say, "The view persists both in the media and the general public that gardens are just comforting or jolly, rather than artistically inspiring."" They make that sound like a bad thing. Now, I don't mean to be hard on them; I think they manage to be sufficiently hard on themselves.

The manifesto goes on, regarding British gardens: "How sad to see a brave and ambitious heritage in gardens abandoned. No amount of clever planting nor any number of tastefully calming gardens can compensate for the loss of that more vigorous attitude."*

The founders talk about the glory days of early Victorian times when "gardens played a major part in the arts and were a significant arena for discussions of taste, the nature of creativity, philosophy and politics"*—the vigorous attitude that has lamentably been lost, I presume.

Having travelled through much of Europe and North America, I can say that my observation of British gardens confirms that they have set a very fine standard for the rest of us. Vigorous attitudes or not, I have never seen their efforts to create beauty in the garden as anything other than spectacular and definitely inspiring. Indeed, we have a lot of catching up to do. Their gardens are steeped in experience going back for generations—a heritage that, to this outsider's eye, is alive and well, so I don't think they need to be so self-critical.

Anyway, let the ThinkinGardens people cultivate vigorous attitudes and weighty discussions. I will continue to trek over there, holding their gardens in the highest esteem. And I will continue to hum "Carolina in My Mind" while reflecting on my incredible British gardening experience.

*ThinkinGardens manifesto, www.thinkingardens.co.uk.

What Value a Garden?

"All human wealth is from the earth."
—**Margaret Atwood,**
Conservation Foundation address, 2006

I recently had the pleasure of hearing Margaret Atwood, arguably Canada's greatest living author, speak on the topic, "Taking the Earth's Temperature," a discussion of global warming and the heated debate it engenders. It was basically heavy stuff, but stuff we need to hear nonetheless if we're going to get off our collective butt and get really serious about the environment.

As a consuming society, we spend a lot of time hoping that the price of gas will not go up. Think of the fortunes that have been invested in the Alberta oil sands in hopes that we will find plentiful domestically produced oil. Atwood offered a useful illustration for those of us who live in hope that there will never be another oil crisis. She told the story of King Midas, who "was granted a wish, and he wished that everything he touched might turn to gold. Everything did turn to gold, including any food he tried to eat and any water he tried to drink. He starved to death."

Since then, I have reflected on King Midas and his fate while toiling in my garden. Hoeing, digging, pruning and planting—all my favourite jobs—allow me the luxury of letting my mind wander; I can even forget how hopeless it is to be a Toronto Maple Leafs hockey fan. Alas, I was born here and this is my lot in life.

But I will take the hand dealt to me and love it to bits,

because in the big picture even being a Leafs fan is not really so bad. (Being a loser has an upside on occasion; it makes the wins so much sweeter.) As I work, I think of all the things I wish for on an ongoing basis: good health, happy kids and a place to live that is clean, safe and pollution-free.

Of all of the issues that have risen in the public consciousness and now fill the media, the one that gives me the greatest concern is the current state of our environment. Here, we can hardly afford to fail. Future generations depend on us to act smartly and act now.

I am reminded of the many failures I have had in the garden, and all that I have learned from them over the years. In spite of the disappointments, there is always next season, and a new opportunity to push the horticultural envelope, to unwittingly kill a few more plants or succeed so wildly that I have to cut the growth back. But where the environment is concerned, we cannot afford the luxury of making a lot of mistakes. Instead, we need to rework our lifestyles, values and standards in ways that will have a positive—and immediate—impact.

Atwood closed her remarks speech at the Conservation Foundation with this, "Instead of turning life into gold, we have the chance to turn gold back into life—good water, fine air, healthy soil, clean energy. I hope we will all avail ourselves of that chance, while we still can."

Who is in a better position to do all the above than those of us who tend the earth?

I consider it a modern gardener's calling.

Farms and Gardens

"That was the best garden," he said, "which produced the most roots and fruits; and that water was most to be prized which contained most fish."

–Hester Lynch Piozzi, quoting Samuel Johnson,
Anecdotes of the Late Samuel Johnson (1786)

CHAPTER 48

It has taken me 50 years, but finally I have a home in the country. Mary and I moved here a mere year ago. Surrounded by farms, I now bump into farmers every time I pump gas at the local station. I chat it up with farmers over a burger at Sam's Restaurant about two kilometres down the road. I even have a brother-in-law next door who proudly calls himself a full-time farmer.

It's handy, having this rich resource next door and down the street. Whenever I need advice about the land, I know where to go. And when I come back home, I usually have a dozen cobs of corn in the car as proof of where I have been. In this first year of living in my new four-hectare (10-acre) garden, I have learned that farmers and gardeners have a whole lot in common, especially where stewardship of the land is concerned.

For example, I wanted to sow some clover this fall as a "green manure" to enhance the soil quality in my veggie garden. I tilled the earth in October and was all set to sow the clover seed when I thought better of it. I would talk to my neighbour Guy just to be sure. "The best time to sow clover is in the first two weeks of April," said Guy. "You just spread the seed on the surface of the soil and the last few frosts of spring will drive the seed down for you. Then we will get lots of spring rain. No need to rake it or cultivate. Just let nature do her work." It's that easy? I said to myself. I let on to Guy that I knew this all along and just needed confirmation.

Dan Needles, author of the great Canadian *Wingfield Farm* series, tells the story of a farmer who was talking with a new neighbour who had escaped the city for the country life.

"Why are there so many rocks on the farms around here?" asked the newbie farmer.

"They're there to knock the soil off your implements as you plow the fields," replied the farmer.

"And why is that guy over there piling his up like that?" asked the inquisitive city boy, pointing across the concession road.

Said the farmer, "Oh, that. Well, he just took delivery of those and he'll be spreading them any time now."

As I have learned, farmers on average have an above-average sense of humour. And they don't take themselves so seriously that they can't laugh at themselves, or each other. And while farmers may have fun with city folk—and vice versa—they have much to teach.

To grow a healthy crop of anything and to grow it well takes time, experience, planning, no end of patience and lots of hard work. Not to mention a large measure of faith that the rains will come—and go—and the sun will shine on a timely basis.

Try to farm or garden without a large measure of faith and you are in for frustrating days. Bring together the soil, water, sun and a packet of seeds and you have a risk that is worth taking. I think gardeners and farmers should get along very well, like fishermen and hunters do. Hikers and campers. You get the idea. The farmers I know have generally come from farming families. Many have made a living on the same land for generations. None of them look at their work as a short-term job, a rung in the ladder to somewhere greater. They have arrived and the land is their best friend.

It only makes sense, then, that farmers respect soil and water for the future income they represent. Modern farming practices call for less disruption of the soil than years ago, a reduction in the use of chemicals and a long-term view to soil quality and productivity.

As a gardener, I plan on picking their brains for a long time yet.

My Feet on the Desk

*"You never achieve real success
unless you like what you are doing."*

—Dale Carnegie

I was talking to my good friend Bob the other day on the phone. We had some serious business to discuss. He runs a plastics company that makes yogurt containers, and my business is talking about gardening. You might wonder what we have in common.

Bob is not only a successful businessman but is also more environmentally responsible than almost anyone I know, so we share an interest in both business and nature.

Pondering the beautiful weather on this fine Friday, we reflected on the fact that many of our business associates were out golfing. Said Bob, "Why is it that I feel guilty if I take the afternoon off to go home and garden, but these guys have no problem going golfing instead of working?"

"Good question," I said. I thought I was the only one who felt pangs of guilt when I went home on a workday to stake the tomatoes.

I have heard golfers say they get a lot of business done over a game. I guess between swings there are those moments when you can grab a quick conversation; maybe near the 18th hole you get lucky and bag a verbal confirmation for the order. I don't know.

CHAPTER 49

My limited experience on the golf course has taught me that there is little time for anything other than the frenetic walking across the fairway from the left rough to the right and back again, all in an effort to keep ahead of the golfers who keep whacking balls over my head. (Why do they bother making the fairway look so nice when I so seldom get to play on it? Wouldn't it make more sense to put the fairway on the margins and the rough in the middle? Or is it just me?)

I am reminded of the advice I received from my friend Evan Church, a retired retail executive with the Hudson's Bay Company. Evan sat on the board of advisers of my little company for quite a few years. One of the first questions that he had for me was, "How much time do you spend with your feet on your desk?"

At the time, I thought it was a rather audacious question. How was I to get anything done with my feet on the desk? And what would staff think if they walked by and saw me sitting there, hands behind my head, feet on the desk, taking it easy? This was hardly the image I was trying to project.

Some explanation was in order. Evan expanded on the question with this, "Everyone who runs a business needs to be thinking about where they are going with it. The next month, year, three years. Who is thinking about the strategy if the boss isn't doing it? And where is the best place to do it?"

Thus began my lesson on "Strategic Thinking 101" courtesy of my new friend.

The garden was the perfect place to "put my feet on the

desk" as it turned out. Staking the tomatoes, hoeing weeds, planting the annuals and sowing seeds—all these activities suit themselves perfectly to the task of thinking.

Perhaps it is the soil. Or the sun. Or the satisfaction that comes from labouring over so-called menial tasks in an effort to grow a plant. It may have something to do with the creative endeavour of making a garden.

I have learned that my time in the garden is precious for the many ideas that I grow there. At the end of a productive session, my head is full of them.

Gardening or golfing. Sailing or fishing. Hiking or cross-country skiing. Does it really make a difference? Probably not, but I have learned what works best for me. As to how much time you should spend with your feet on the desk, Evan says 20 percent. His professional track record speaks for itself, so I think I will stick with that—and not worry about feeling guilty.

Private Gardens, Public Tours

"Don't step on the flowers!"

–Paul Williamson
williamsongroup.com

If there is an organization that promotes tours of private gardens, I would like to apply to become their spokesperson. As I travel across Canada, I am made aware of a growing number of these wonderful events and it seems to me that having more them would only do us good.

The idea is to open up your yard—front and/or back—to an organized, self-guided tour put together by some well-meaning group in your community (garden club, hospital auxiliary, etc.). Guests pay a small fee to see some beautiful, carefully chosen gardens; the organization (which is almost always not-for-profit) raises money and awareness for its cause; and hosts who open their gardens put on their best garden-face for the event. It's a win-win-win all round.

I have been on both the guest and host end of this stick and have enjoyed both. To be truthful, I am probably a better guest than host-I won't talk your ear off and I wear the right kind of shoes, the ones that do not puncture holes in your lawn. When you go on one of these tours, you will often pick up design ideas that you can incorporate into your own garden. You will see plants that may suit your garden situation and, in some cases, you get to talk to the homeowner/gardener, which provides an excellent opportunity to pick their brains and benefit from their experience and passion for gardening. If the garden you are touring happens to be maintained professionally, you'll see how the pros do it. This can be good

if you are looking for, say, different pruning techniques.
Apart from the plants, there are water features, garden statuary, birdbaths, sun dials or other forms of art that add interest and tell the story of both the garden and its owners.

You won't always agree with the look achieved in each garden, but that is one of the beauties of the thing. A garden tour opens your eyes to garden concepts you may not have seen or considered before. It may also answer some questions that have vexed you about your own garden. For instance, how do you have a good-looking garden and a dog at the same time? Where do young children fit into a garden theme? How can I hide an unsightly composter while having it conveniently located to the kitchen? What can I grow in the shade?

On the host side, one of the great benefits is the terrific people you meet. I find that "garden tourers" are by nature thoughtful, considerate and very complimentary. However, if you are asked to put your garden on a tour, make sure that the organizers will have a steward stationed at your home from the beginning to the end of the tour. They will make sure that people don't trample your garden or otherwise abuse the privilege of being there. You can choose to be on hand to answer questions or go indoors, as you please.

If you have never been on a garden tour, you may be surprised at how interesting a stranger's backyard can be. It is a little like looking into their bedroom; this is private space that they did not design in the first place for public viewing. But the pride, commitment and love lavished on the space are usually very evident. And a joy to behold. Most garden tours happen in late spring, so mark your calendars and get your walking shoes ready. Inspiration awaits.

Hitting a Wall

"A life spent making mistakes is not only more honorable but more useful than a life spent doing nothing."

—George Bernard Shaw

Three years ago, my wife Mary and I decided to build a house on her family farm, just 10 minutes north of the town of Unionville where we had lived for over 20 years. What I liked most about the idea was that I could finally create my dream garden without space limitations. The first thing I did was to walk into the property from the road until I arrived at what I thought was a reasonable distance to build a nice garden. It worked out to four hectares (10 acres).

From there, I went crazy with design ideas. I would sketch vistas and corners of my new landscape on onion skin paper, creating layers of designs that became more elaborate with every page. I doodled and sketched on the back of boarding passes while on airplanes, and made lists of my favourite plants on the back of the order of service while sitting in church (my mother would have killed me for that one!).

Everything seemed to be going along swimmingly, until I tried to pull all my design concepts together into one cohesive plan. My first attempt resulted in a secret garden, a butterfly garden and a koi pond all connected within the same space. The problem was there was no logic or flow to the scheme. I had hit a wall.

Here I was with more than 20 years' experience of professional gardening behind me. I had designed about 500 gardens for clients of our family firm, Weall and Cullen Nurseries. I had written a book and numerous newspaper articles on the subject yet, faced with all of the potential of an empty canvas, this "artist" was at a loss as to where to begin.

At that point, I happened to attend the annual symposium of the Perennial Plant Association in the United States, where Gordon Hayward was speaking about garden design. Gordon is a tall, quiet man, with a very gentle way about him. By his own admission, he was trained as an English major, not a garden designer. But he has found his niche in garden design. Listening to him, I knew that he was the guy who could help me break the dam of ideas that was holding me back from transforming my field of dreams into reality.

He talked about creating an agenda for your garden, about having an overall plan that featured paths, around which everything revolved.

He talked about the role of structure in the garden, "Boulders make a good spine in the garden," he said, which was good news for me as my dad had given me four truckloads of beautiful cut fieldstone to use in my new garden scheme. On the subject of moving heavy stones around the garden, Gordon's advice was to use a poet to do the job, not a cowboy. His point was that a scratched and dented rock used as a feature in your garden would look anything but natural, "The ruse is up!" he'd say. A poet would use his soft hands to handle the stone with respect.

Where paths were concerned, Gordon favoured the use of pea gravel. "It lights up a dark space and announces your arrival with a crunch."

I liked everything that he had to say.

Gordon agreed to come to our site, which actually has much in common with his native Vermont growing zone, except that we don't have any mountains.

After two days of walking, measuring and talking about the property, he got to work on the design. Within a few weeks, he sent me a full set of drawings that incorporated his paths, many of the ideas we had discussed during his visit, and many of the ideas I had put on paper before we met.

I was off to the races with so much to do and so little to time to do it. I got help from my friend Rudy and we rolled up our sleeves and got to work; we dug and planted, built stone walls, installed a water feature, moved soil to create berms and generally laboured like gardeners obsessed.

My garden is still very young, a baby really. With just two years of progress behind me, I look forward to the next 10 and 20 years as the garden that we envisioned unfolds, matures and no doubt changes in surprising ways.

I am more than satisfied with the plan, and implementing it is my idea of fun. Indeed, I have found a big new sandbox to play in.

Mary, Mary

If you have read the earlier chapters of this book, you know I have made reference to my four kids. Lynn, the creative, energetic, oh-so-passionate knitter; Heather, our landscape architect in the making (currently at the University of Guelph); and Ben, the car fanatic.

Our third child, Emma, also has some very special talents, not the least of which is photography. She loves to shoot outdoors and, proud parent that I am, I think she has a particular talent in that regard.

It is with her permission then that I conclude this book on personal garden reflections with a photo essay. This is a personal reflection on the current state of our environment. Here it is, with many thanks to Emma:

Mary, Mary quite contrary,

How does your garden grow?

Or does it?

Mark Cullen was raised in the gardening business and worked with his father, Len, in the family firm, Weall & Cullen. Mark's passion is communicating the gardening message and he is in high demand as a public speaker—"I love to connect with Canadians who love to garden," he says. Over the past 25 years, he has written 17 garden books including the bestselling Canadian gardening book, A Greener Thumb. Mark is a regional columnist for Gardening Life magazine and has recently written for the Globe and Mail.

A popular broadcaster, Mark can be heard every Saturday morning answering gardening questions on The Garden Show on Newstalk 1010 CFRB in Toronto and, on Wednesday mornings,

he co-hosts the gardening segment on CTV's Canada AM with funny-man Jeff Hutchison. For five years, Mark hosted the HGTV show, Mark Cullen Gardening, and is now the host of HGTV's new environmental show, Green Force.

Mark is the resident gardening expert for Home Hardware, and an advocate for Green Earth Garden Products and slow release, organic based lawn fertilizer C.I.L. Golfgreen.

When not gardening, working or driving his Ford Model A, he promotes the excellent work of S.H.A.R.E. Agricultural Foundation. Mark lives in Stouffville, Ont., on a country property with his wife, Mary, and four children.

Notes

Notes

Notes

The quotes that you see in this book have come from a variety of sources. Most of them I have collected over time from articles that I have read or people that I know. In each case I have given the appropriate credit.

There are two sources of some quotes that deserve special mention. One is the book *The Quotable Gardener* edited by Charles Elliott and published by The Lyons Press.
It is an excellent source of short garden quotes.

The other source is the monthly publication called *Green Prints - The Weeder's Digest*. This is a wonderful compilation of gardening stories that do not have anything to do with the practical aspects of the subject, and everything to do with the soft side. That is to say that each issue will make you laugh and perhaps even cry. It provides insight into the psychology of gardening and the reasons why we do it.
I look forward to each issue and reserve a special place beside my bed for it.

To learn more about GreenPrints, go to greenprints.com or contact them at
Green Prints
P.O. Box 1355
Fairview, North Carolina
28730

My thanks to Pat Stone, the editor at Green Prints.